RELUCTANT COOK

THE NON-COOK'S COOKBOOK

Illustrations by the author

JANE GIBB

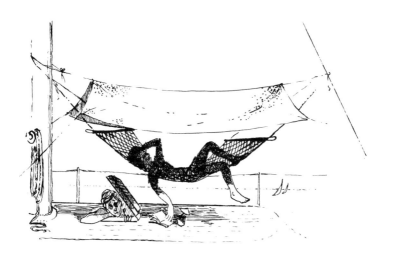

ADLARD COLES NAUTICAL
LONDON

Adlard Coles Nautical
an imprint of A & C Black (Publishers) Ltd
35 Bedford Row, London, WC1R 4JH

First published in Great Britain by
Adlard Coles Nautical 1991

A CIP catalogue record for this book is available from
the British Library.

Typeset by Latimer Trend & Company Ltd, Plymouth
in 10pt Helvetica Light
Printed and bound in Great Britain by Hollen Street Press, Slough.

CONTENTS

To John,

who got me into this fine mess

ACKNOWLEDGEMENTS

First to the many sailing friends who sent me recipes to consider, my sincere thanks. Not just for their letters but also the memorable meals afloat in quiet anchorages, dedicated to research and contemplation of the universe. For those who don't see their contribution in print please know that it was only from lack of space, and that *all* recipes submitted have gone into my own personal edition. Next I acknowledge the generosity of the companies I approached when researching products and equipment.

Thanks go to Melissa McGinn of Philadelphia, PA. for her professional advice with Desserts; we had fun, too. Also to friends who, for the last year or so, have tolerated my increasingly eccentric behaviour with affectionate indulgence; my grateful thanks – though I can't promise to improve now it's all over.

I owe a special debt of appreciation to my editor Janet Murphy, whose enthusiasm and gentle guidance have steered me past the many pitfalls in the diuretic throes of publishing my first book.

Not the least to my husband, whose eagle eye as in-house proof reader, fierce critique and even fiercer championship I value beyond price; to him my love and gratitude.

Finally, loving thanks are due to my parents, Ken and Trixie Buckel of Cannes, who started it all. To my father for his grammatical guidance and thesaurean advice, and to my witty mother, who never taught me to cook.

INTRODUCTION

I have many amazing talents, as I am always reminding my husband, but cooking isn't one of them. I haven't liked cooking for as far back as I can remember and it hasn't got any better with time. All I have done over the years is to accumulate easy, fail-proof recipes that will get me out of trouble and out of the kitchen with the least trauma.

This little book is the result of that accumulation and is put together to help those other poor souls who, like myself, find preparing and cooking food a daily grind. This chore is so dreadful that its mere contemplation is enough to send us into a blind funk. We realise, however, that if we don't do it ourselves then probably no one else will either, and starvation will result.

But we non-cooks like to eat, don't we? Not for us the nutrition pill of Huxley's *Brave New World*. So when we can't persuade someone else to do the honours – and I can sniff out an invitation to dine as quick as a shark smells blood – we must turn to and make the best of it.

If you are an enthusiastic cook, if you thrill to the challenge of 'What shall we have for dinner tonight?', if, for you, there is no greater solace than to spend an uninterrupted afternoon in the kitchen devising some new gastronomic delight – read no further. For though it will boost your self-esteem, you will only come to despise me more than I despise myself. You might even know me, in which case all my cheap tricks will be apparent to you and I will have to suffer your withering scorn when next we meet. I couldn't bear it.

If you have bought this book or had it given to you, I am grateful; I have a boat to support and every penny counts. If you can't use it, give it to some deserving, harassed sea-wife who may find within its modest pages a few crumbs of comfort or even something to feed the brutes on the foredeck. If you are that harassed sea-wife you've probably got enough cook books to fill a good-sized trunk. For someone who claims to disdain cooking I have a collection of cook books that would be the envy of the local catering college, but it's like searching for the Holy Grail. You hope each new one will give you that key to culinary competence, and each time you're disappointed.

Have you noticed how the cover pictures always have bright shiny cooks in their bright shiny kitchens with a smile a mile wide doing the thing they like best? It's so depressing, if you're a cook-o-phobe, to be confronted with that degree of bludgeoning enthusiasm. To make matters worse, the authors are always terrifyingly qualified, with years of training and experience, for writing about cooking. Me? I even delegate heating the water for tea.

You'll also have noticed too, that these aficionados can be so naively presuming. 'When you prepare artichokes for Salade Catalannaise . . .' For WHAT? I have never prepared artichokes in my life and I don't intend to start now. I leave that to those wizards of the kitchen who delight in whisking up a cheeky little item with one well-manicured hand while not spilling a drop of the dry Martini held in the other. I fall flat on my face with admiration; long may they live – and invite me to their table.

I used to think I hated cooking, but on reflection I realise my feelings fall just short of hatred. If you hate something then you never enjoy doing it. Occasionally – just occasionally – however, I do actually enjoy making a dish that turns out well. When the plates come back polished, when I have eaten my own share with pleasure, or when someone bothers to compliment me on the meal, I feel a nice little glow. I am pleased with myself and I think everyone should have a chance to feel like that too, once in a while.

People will tell you that things get easier the more you do them. Lies, damned lies! Those of us who don't like cooking have learned that it gets no better with repetition. Are they really trying to tell us that dental visits, tax returns and labour pains are more fun each time round? Rot! There are many interesting ways of getting tired and cooking isn't one of them. Cooking bores us non-cooks. We would really rather be sipping a tincture, clad only in a sarong while contemplating a brilliant sunset from the afterdeck of some teak-laid extravagance of yesteryear.

The reality differs sadly. As the time approaches for yet another meal we feel the panic rising. Friends who cook for fun (can this be true?) advise us to make a list, plan the meals for a week – or a month – ahead. But we can't bear to contemplate the thought before time, consequently we leave it to the last moment. We'll tell you what we're having when it's on the table – if we can find a name for it. Sometimes, during the day, the spectre of a meal to be produced that evening will drift luridly before our eyes and threaten to ruin the day until, with immense strength of character, we force it from our mind.

Those same dear friends urge us to take up night-school. But if you suffer from cook-o-phobia you don't *want* to get better. Not for us the jolly evening classes in 'Gordon Blur', our attention span is far too short – like three minutes . . . on a good day. Besides, if we improved our skills it would mean doing even more cooking than now; friends would get to hear of our progress and start coming to visit us instead and invitations to dine out might decline – and that's NOT the idea at all. After all, you are not going to be dragged out in search of Salade Catalannaise if you can come up with the goods yourself. So we play it low key.

Meanwhile, take heart, all you reluctant cooks out there – help is at hand. I have no diplomas, nor have I ever catered for crowned heads or corporations over the years. However, I have scraped together just enough skill to get by with a modicum of success and a minimum of effort. The essence of my sufferings, torn from my very soul, is distilled in this mighty tome. Scary, isn't it?

You will find nothing exotic within these pages. Leave that for when your mate is feeling romantic and you can wangle a meal out for yourself. Here you will find simple every day dishes to make afloat, or ashore; maybe like me you're just not organised enough to cope with the difference. One location just moves a little more than the other, that's all.

I am indebted to the many fellow sufferers – and even those who like to cook – who have given freely of their 'Four Squares' (Secret Surefire Success Standbys). If you recognise something that looks like one of your own recipes without a credit to you, my apologies; I've probably forgotten from whom I stole it!

VICTUALLING

The Prevailing Conditions

'Sail away with me' he says, as you swoon against his manly chest. What he doesn't say but what he really means is . . . Serve him up a continuous supply of appetising, sustaining, plentiful nosh at regular intervals plus a succession of snacks and nibbles and interesting things to drink. What he also neglects to add is that the facilities from which you will be asked to bring forth these culinary miracles would make a tinker's kitchen look like a *Bon Viveur* film set. Add to these difficulties the fact that your work surface will probably be less than two square feet, leaning at ever changing angles between 15° and 45° in any plane, whilst heaving and swooping like a flight simulator.

On the bulkhead in my galley at eye-level there is a small notice urging DON'T PANIC. I try to heed it when possible, but some-

... apparently in orbit

times it needs the back-up of action. Like the time out in the Atlantic swells when, looking up suddenly from my pans, I was aware that beyond the galley port there was nothing except sky. For a moment I concluded, thoughtfully, that we must be in orbit. Then the boat rolled a little and I saw with horror that we were perched at the top of an enormous wall of water. I realised at that moment what it must be like to face the Cresta run with a lunatic in charge. We whooshed down into the trough and the bottom fell out of my boots. I stared spellbound as we were swept inexorably up the side of the next wall of evil green water, teetering at its crest before accelerating down the other side into another trough, like a roller coaster.

At this point I decided 'Ignorance was Bliss' and, until the sea behaved itself again, I closed the curtains firmly, tightened the galley bum-strap and refused to look out except from the cockpit. From that viewpoint, funnily enough, things didn't seem half so bad. I think it was the shock of the unexpected.

You will not always have total possession of the galley area. For instance, when they start tinkering with that mutinous mass of metal known as the engine, the companionway steps have to be removed. This converts the galley into the engine room. The space will be filled with hunched bodies, the air with blue smoke, part nautical language, part burnt cooking.

Don't naively expect that this absolves you from your culinary duties, however. To the contrary, heads will suddenly appear asking if lunch/tea/dinner etc. is ready, and faces will register aggrieved innocence or incredulous disbelief at your incompetence that you've not managed to throw even a simple banquet together while they've been virtually re-inventing the internal combustion engine. Don't even bother to argue, just suggest that if you don't get your galley back in less than five minutes it will be far too late to start preparing and cooking anything and you will all just have to go ashore to eat at that nice little place you spotted on the way in/on the last trip/in the guide book or recommended by the big blonde on the other boat who eats there every night. With a bit of luck you might just get a meal out.

Galleys also have their own idiosyncrasies. The pan or the food item you want will always be under or behind something else which you don't want, in the deepest, farthest part of any locker — assuming you know which locker to consult in the first place. On one tack or the other, the sink won't empty. When the hatch is open there will be an annoying little drip that trickles down your perpetually bent neck. There will be a locker corner that lies in wait for you, inflicting a series of vicious little jabs that will only reveal themselves later in the privacy of the heads as purple/

yellow patches in the most unlikely places, making you look like a battle victim – which, of course, you are.

Other minor distractions will be inevitable, like your presence being demanded on deck IMMEDIATELY to hold her head to wind while he does a spot of fancy foredeck footwork. Or hauling up the anchor and holding on to it until your circulation threatens to give up while he does yet another circuit of the bay on a quest for better holding. All are par for the course.

But you wouldn't listen to your mother and here you are, tied up with a sailor. The only thing to do if escape is impossible (or undesirable) is . . . face the facts and get on with it.

Stores for a cosy weekend on *Fluffy Duck* can all be prepared at various odd times during the week, put from the fridge/freezer straight into the cool box and away you go. Nothing more to do but dish it out periodically, perhaps warmed first, and keep the kettle on the boil. The rubbish returns in the cool box. No problems. The fun begins when he starts talking about that long cruise he's always promised you when the kids grew up. It's then you realise it's physically impossible; there's not enough space to prepare, cook, clear away and wash up, let alone to store the vast amounts of food that will be needed, but like the bumble bee you'll get on and do it anyway. I bet Cleopatra never had these problems trolling down the Nile.

Starting again

It's no good going to sea for any period, let alone an extended cruise, expecting to behave the same way as one did in a comfortable 'des res' in middle suburbia. It demands a whole rethink of the victualling problem. The aim is to provide food which is appetising, nourishing and plentiful for more than a weekend. The food must be easy to store, need little or no refrigeration, and have a minimum of inedible residue. In other words, it must have little packaging, be biodegradable if possible, not contain too many parts you don't eat, and there must be few tins.

The diet must include plenty of fresh fruit and vegetables. Back in 1928 E. G. Martin said in *Deep Water Cruising* that '. . . meals should be wholesome, varied and as attractive as possible.' The same holds good today but now, with the new laws on not dumping rubbish at sea, the honest sailor will be lumbered with a lot of garbage to carry back to a suitable shore disposal point. 'No Dumping at Sea' means that tins, the sailors' standby, are now a menace as, once empty, they will have to be kept to be dumped at a suitable point ashore. In my humble opinion very little tinned food comes up to home cooking and don't you quickly tire of the eternal meatballs and carrot one-pot? But tins do have their uses – the aim here is to keep them to a minimum. So, where has that got us?

1. What food to take.
2. How to store it.
3. How to cook it.
4. How to keep inedible residue to the minimum.

Take No. 1 of the above first.

What food to take

What food can you take on board that will last for a month and require no refrigeration? Well, reluctantly, meat has to go for a start. But you won't miss it, I promise you and you can save your meat-teeth for those romantic trips ashore.

Meat is one of the prime causes of tummy upsets. As it has specialised storage requirements, do you really need the extra hassle at sea? Ideally meat should have a fridge to itself, as the raw product should not come into contact with any other food. This is difficult enough ashore with a decent size fridge but well nigh impossible on the average boat. As for tinned meat, I've not eaten any that tasted of anything worth mentioning, and besides, we're aiming to keep away from the tins as much as possible.

FRUIT AND VEGETABLES

Plenty of fresh fruit and vegetables are a must to provide good nutrition and a boost for moral. It restores a sense of normality to be able to sink your teeth into an apple with one hand on the helm while gazing on a limitless horizon. All the citrus fruits provide vital vitamins and are good 'wake-up food'. Bananas are sustaining and good night-watch nosh. White cabbage can be eaten fresh or cooked. Potatoes, carrots, swede, parsnips are obvious choices, but don't neglect the more exotic vegetables like yams, sweet potatoes, aubergine, squash, celeriac, kohlrabi and mooli which keep well and help make interesting changes (*see* the chapter on Vegetables).

Vegetables that add flavouring, such as onions, mushrooms, peppers and root ginger are useful and all, except the mushrooms, keep well. Dried mushrooms are a good substitute, and they smell delicious – the drying process seems to concentrate their aroma. Garlic is a natural intestinal disinfectant, will shift the gunge in colds and other respiratory infections and helps reduce blood pressure – this could be the most valuable vegetable on board.

There's no point in listing all the fruit and vegetables you might buy. Just stock as much as you have stowage space for, and then more, especially extra fruit. It always surprises me how hungry we are in the first few days of a cruise, and what looked like full bins soon show gaps. Little and often seems to be the guide to a quiet stomach.

'OK,' I hear you say, 'but if there's no meat, where's the protein?' In the GRPs, of course.

GRAINS, ROOTS and PULSES

In various combos – any two of three – grains, roots and pulses will provide you with the protein your body needs. Add eggs and cheese and you have more than enough protein to build a Fastnet crew. If you catch fish along the way, you have a bonus.

Grains (and cereals) make up the bulk of staple food for the world. As well as providing protein, they contain iron, calcium potassium and phosphorus, all essential elements in a good diet. If you're still not convinced that you won't go short of something, read Rose Elliot's *Beanfeast* (Fontana). My son was delighted when he learned that baked beans on toast (Pulse + Grain) make a perfect protein meal.

Grains include wholewheat which has a lovely chewy texture, barley with its thickening properties, bulgur or cracked wheat which needs no cooking, oats, rice (black, white or brown and all shades in between), maize, millet and rye. All the grains come as whole or rolled, coarse or fine, or milled into flour, which multiplies its uses. Into this category I also put things like semolina, couscous and buckwheat, which is really a seed, with its distinctive flavour.

Roots are all the root vegetables you can think of: potatoes, carrots, parsnips, kohlrabi, swede, yams, sweet potatoes, eddoes, etc.

Pulses, which include dried peas, beans and lentils, are a cheap source of protein with the added advantage of being low in fat but high in fibre. They are formed in two halves. Generally, beans – and some peas – have skins holding the two halves together, while lentils and split peas have been skinned and are split in two.

Beans are available in such variety today from the average supermarket that they are almost beyond counting, from the deep red kidney bean and its little cousin, the round red adzuki bean, through the fat white butter bean and the pale smaller haricot, to the mottled pinto and borlotti beans and the cowboys' favourite, the aptly named black-eyed bean with its distinctive black eye on the cream marble skin – and there are many more. Their different colourings and shapes add interest to dishes. They also come ready packed in colourful mixes in the supermarket, which is probably the best way to buy them if you don't want to buy a sack of each individually.

Beans can be sprouted, though the most popular bean to sprout is Mung, a small dark green bean which will produce those succulent crunchy sprouts you know from Chinese cookery. Sprouted beans increase their bulk many times and likewise their food value. Sprouting beans afloat is very worthwhile as it can provide fresh vegetables indefinitely (*see* the chapter on Vegetables).

Other pulses are the split peas and lentils, large and small. They come in yellow, red, green, orange and brown, and are useful for adding body to a dish. Lentils have the advantage of not requiring a presoak or rapid boiling. In fact they benefit from gentle cooking, and a cup of the familiar red lentils to feed two people will cook in little more than 10 minutes.

Caution: There is a price to be paid for the convenience of dried beans in as much as they *must boil rapidly for the first ten minutes of cooking*, after the preparatory soak. This is because some, though not all, contain an enzyme that may sometimes cause serious stomach upset if eaten undercooked.

But let's get this in perspective – you would not dream of serving pork or poultry undercooked. Likewise, there are some simple precautions that must be observed with beans, and the necessary high cooking temperatures can easily be achieved by using a pressure cooker which also reduces cooking time (*see* Cooking beans (the easy way) in the chapter on Vegetables).

Nuts can be put with seeds into the Pulse/Bean category. They are high in protein and have distinctive flavours making them a valuable addition to any store cupboard. The most commonly used nuts are, I suppose, peanuts. These are usually to be found already roasted and salted. If you have a wholefood store near you, you may be able to find plain peanuts. It really doesn't matter which you use in savoury recipes except that you need to adjust the salt level. You can always rinse the salted ones for sweet recipes. Chopped mixed nuts can be bought quite cheaply from most supermarkets. These are quite good enough for toppings, nut crumbles and burgers. Almonds, walnuts, hazelnuts and brazils have distinctive flavourings and are best used separately. Flaked almonds are usually cheaper than whole, taste just as good and go further. They are nice as a garnish on top of well drained spinach or to throw in to stir fried vegetables at the last minute.

Caution: Unlike pulses, which are dried and have a long shelf-life, nuts with their high oil content go rancid quickly and produce 'free radicals', substances known to cause ageing! So buy your nuts in small quantities from a reliable source with a quick turnover and use them quickly.

DAIRY PRODUCTS

These, I grant, can be a problem without refrigeration, but this is where the supermarket packaging comes into its own.

Cheese should be bought vacuum-packed in small amounts and stored in the coolest place – below the waterline, probably. Plan to use each portion within a day or two. It will keep well enough without refrigeration if tightly wrapped in greaseproof paper in a sealed container. If, despite your efforts, it goes runny, wipe it off with vinegar. This holds good for cheese that's gone a bit mouldy, too. Just trim off the mould, wipe with vinegar and use for cooking if it's become too strong.

Parmesan is a hard dry cheese originally from Parma but now made in other parts of northern Italy. It is more expensive than ordinary hard cheeses but a little goes a long way. With a distinctive flavour, it is a traditional topping grated over many pasta dishes. Because of its very dry nature it keeps well without refrigeration wrapped in a muslin or similar cloth and stored in an airtight bin in as cool a place as possible.

Caution: Do make sure the bin is air tight or, like George's friend in *Three Men in a Boat* (J. K. Jerome), the smell may insidiously invade the atmosphere and defy identification, causing panic, mayhem and even calls to abandon ship. Parmesan comes ready grated in a tub for those of a nervous disposition.

Blue-veined cheeses keep fairly well in a cool place and just go on getting bluer. Wrapping any cheese in a muslin cloth dampened with vinegar will help to preserve it in good condition. It should then be overwrapped in greaseproof paper before being stored in an airtight bin in a cool place.

About the only processed cheese worth bothering with, in my opinion, is *The Laughing Cow*. Somehow the manufacturers have managed to make it taste less 'plastic' than the others and it keeps well without refrigeration. If they would just provide us with a perfect way of opening those little foil parcels . . . I end up having to do it for everyone or else squashy pieces of silver paper keep turning up for days afterwards. Edam, with its wax overcoat, keeps well but needs a little jazzing up with ground pepper. The cream cheeses, having a higher fat content, need to be eaten quickly once opened, though the sealed tubs keep well.

Margarine keeps better than butter and **cooking fat** seems to keep for ages. Tinned **butter** keeps well too. I have been able to buy New Zealand butter in 1 lb (450 g) tins; the trouble is, once opened you have to use the whole pound quickly, which is a lot of butter without refrigeration. In a cool bilge, butter will keep for one week. After that use it for cooking for two days. Rancid fats are bad for you. Adding 1 tsp of salt to unsalted butter (mix well and keep in a cool place) extends its life.

Milk can be a problem in that it has a tendency to slop about and smells disgusting if spilt into inaccessible corners or on absorbent materials. A wash with a mild bleach solution seems to be the only answer to the smell. Cartons of long-life milk are invaluable and the small cartons help limit the amount that can go off, get spilt or wasted. If you haven't already, try to wean your crew off full cream milk and on to skimmed. Then you can use dried milk powder in drinks which makes life far easier – and healthier.

Cream in cartons seems to work just as well as the fresh variety and means that you can offer that little extra touch of luxury to lift a dish out of the ordinary. The cartons come in 7 fl.oz (200 ml) sizes (about 1 cup) of single, double and whipping varieties and shelf-life is about six months. Also useful for pouring over puddings is a 'dessert topping' made with skimmed milk, which claims to have $\frac{1}{3}$ less fat than double cream. It can be used for sweet and savoury cooking and will whip. I think it tastes a bit like melted ice cream on its own and would keep it strictly for pouring over sweet things, where it tastes alright.

Still looking for an alternative to evaporated milk in a tin? Try mixing equal parts of coffee whitener and water. Make half the water fairly warm to melt the powder and top up with cold. It's quite reasonable over a dessert and you can adjust the proportions to suit your own taste but its a bit sickly if made too strong. It's also rather high on calories, fat and sugar.

Eggs will keep well enough for a week or two, just as you get them from the supermarket. If, however, you are planning for longer then you must get your eggs straight from the hen, *unwashed* and *unrefrigerated*. Coat them lightly with cooking oil and turn them top to bottom once a week. The only way to guarantee unrefrigerated eggs is to go direct to a reputable egg farm and arrange to collect them yourself. Most people are fascinated, in this day of hi-tech and hygiene, to hear the reasons for your request and are pleased to be a part of the plan. They will tell their friends how you are dotty enough to want to sail alway from good solid land for that length of time. They could have a point . . .

PACKETS, SACHETS, CARTONS, TUBES, JARS and
READY MEALS

I don't think it's cheating to take along your favourite cake mixes if it covers a weak spot. I cannot make a sponge cake for love nor money, yet I've been shown a thousand times how easy it is. There's something they don't like about the way I do it and sponges come out as tired, thin and mean as a spinster's scowl. These disasters are barely recyclable in a trifle, so I resort to a cake mix. It is worth experimenting to find the ones that have the highest success rates with you and your crew and stick to those. Some supermarkets do their own in plastic packs which take up less space than boxes.

If you have access to a cash-and-carry store, look for catering packs of freeze dried instant mixes. These are made by the big names and come in sweet and savoury forms. For instance, I used to use an excellent steak and kidney mix which only needed to have water added. The disadvantage is that the goods are packaged in large sizes only, and once opened you have to use them in a reasonable time. But I'm talking of weeks not days, so if you are catering for a larger than average crew this might be a worthwhile ploy, or perhaps you know another harassed cook who might be glad to share with you.

If you don't want to bother making your own sauces the average supermarket stocks a bewildering choice of instant dried packet sauces, sweet and savoury, that will speed things along. They are more expensive than making your own and some contain additives I'm not sure about. But I feel they have a place in the galley because they take up little space and the empty packets fold flat.

Many soup mixes can be used at double strength to make a sauce to go over vegetables, pasta or rice. There is also a wide choice of dried 'cook-in' type instant sauces that will do a turn if you are looking for an easy way 'out'.

Look also for cartons to replace tins. Tomatoes, always a useful ingredient, come in cartons, calling themselves 'creamed' which is a little odd as they are pure tomato with nothing added – puréed really. (Cartons, when empty, will hold less desirable items like wet garbage or discarded diesel rags; you can fold over the top to seal in the pong, or fold it flat.)

Colman's, Crosse & Blackwell, Batchelor's and Knorr, among others, make a good range of cooking sauces which, added to rice or pasta make an instant meal. Some claim to have no artificial preservatives if you're concerned about that, but still manage a shelf life of up to nine months. Look for a range of rice based meals with added vegetables and seasoning. Just adding water and simmering for 20 minutes makes the basis for a meal to which you can add your own choice of protein, be it fish, meat, cheese, etc. Good heavy-weather food.

Instant noodles are another boon. They come plain or whole wheat, and most need no more than boiling water poured over and allowed to sit for a few minutes. Use stock or a cube with the boiling water and make your own 'pot noodles'.

No-pre-cook wholewheat lasagna gives excellent results. This comes in sheet form. Allow 25% more liquid as the lasagna absorbs quite a bit but follow the instructions on the packet for a very quick dish.

Instant mashed potato has come a long way and is now hard to tell from the real thing. As a thickener for soups or when you've run out of potatoes or just not in the mood to prepare fresh, instant mash is a boon. Use it to make Potato Pizza (*see* chapter on Vegetables) or to top Shepherd's Pie (*see* chapter on Savouries) as well as the conventional use.

Vacuum-packed foods like garlic sausage, salami and bacon have a reasonable shelf-life without refrigeration. The slim pepperami sausage keeps for six to eight weeks and adds a spice to pilaff, pizza and risotto when you're short on fresh things. You'll find them individually vacuum-wrapped in packs of five. They are a bit high on the no-no's like nitrates but you're not going to live exclusively on the product.

Another situation to cater for, though I hate to mention it, is emergency cooking. I'm not proposing 'Oat Coozine' in the liferaft – that subject has been dealt with by people more qualified than I hope you or I will ever be. I'm talking about the times when the going is really tough and it's all you can do to manage the bare essentials of nature and hope the boat will manage herself. This is where a little cache of instant dried meals will come to the rescue. Good climbing and camping shops usually stock a range of dehydrated ready meals. These vary in their appeal and it's worth trying a selection ashore before making a choice for ship's stores. Most of them just need rehydrating in a pan with water for a few minutes; some only need the addition of boiling water to the opened packet. Eddie Bauer (a US East Coast chain store selling sportswear and equipment) do a superb range of dried meals that we found tasty, satisfying and, most importantly, appealing to the eye. If you get to the other side, or have friends who are coming back, it might be worth asking for supplies.

PASTA!

The non-cook's delight. It's cheap, dry, easy to store, comes in great variety, and doesn't need peeling. It's a doddle to cook –

both sweet and savoury, hot or cold, and there aren't many who won't eat it.

Home-made pasta is as good as home-made bread and nearly as easy to make, but keep that under your hat. Most of the time you will want to use the ready-made dried pastas, but just once in a while when life seems particularly calm, like Wednesday early-closing half way between the Azores and Antigua, you might consider giving it a try. Home-made pasta is particularly delicious and quite unlike the dried product. You can even dry your own which will keep in an air-tight bin. Follow the recipe in the Breads, Cakes and Biscuits chapter and your crew will follow you anywhere.

Dried pasta comes in all shapes and sizes including flat sheets, wholemeal or plain. Shells and twirls hold more sauce and look more attractive than the old fashioned 'elbow' macaroni which still reminds me of school dinners. Pasta can be made with egg and is delicious in thin soups. You will also find pasta flavoured with spinach which turns it green, or carrot which turns it orange; these mixed with plain make an interesting combination, though the colours are more apparent than the flavours.

There is a no-precook wholewheat lasagna which I find very useful. You merely combine the sauce, vegetables, lasagna sheets and cheese in alternating layers ending with the cheese, and cook all together adding some extra liquid (*see* chapter on Savouries).

RICE

Rice is another good basic for all the same reasons as pasta but I'm not going to suggest you have your own paddy field. Rice on its own provides protein and carbohydrates. Served plain it is a perfect complement to many dishes in place of the more traditional potatoes; with the addition of a few vegetables and some seasoning you have a complete meal. Brown rice has more flavour, fibre and protein than white, but sometimes it's nice to ring the changes. An interesting mix is 2:1 brown and white. Start the brown off first as it takes longer to cook. It's worth experimenting with various sorts of rice to appreciate their different qualities if you are not familiar with them.

Wild black rice is really a form of water grass, but the effect of its slim black grains scattered through a dish of white rice is quite dramatic. It's wildly expensive too, but as you only put half a tablespoon of dried grains to a whole bowl of rice the real cost is in pennies. A good squeeze of lemon juice over this rice gives it a nice tang and is a good foil to a hot curry.

Basmati is the Queen of Rice and worth the extra cost. It is a particularly firm rice, isn't gluey and has a delightfully long slim grain. It's well worth using and cooking more than you need for the immediate meal as it is the best rice to use cold, keeping its clean shape and separate grains.

If you're short on rice or want to serve up something different, try adding some red lentils (*see* below) about 10 minutes before the rice is cooked. Proportions don't really matter here, but be sure not to let the lentils overcook and go mushy.

LENTILS

Red lentils will stand on their own as an accompanying vegetable and, to me at least, have the most flavour of all the pulses. The fact that they need no pre-soaking and cook quickly is appealing also. They need only be boiled until just tender, then drained, fluffed up with a fork and dressed with butter and pepper to provide a tasty replacement for potatoes. Added to soups and casseroles they will add bulk and flavour.

Brown lentils have the same qualities as red but some people might be put off by their colour so they are best added to other dishes rather than used on their own.

BUCKWHEAT

Buckwheat is another alternative to potatoes. Take $\frac{1}{3}$ cup of buckwheat and boil gently for 10 minutes in twice the volume of water. Drain and fluff with a fork to allow some steam to escape then coat with 1 tbsp of tahine or peanut butter, some salt and a turn of the pepper mill. You can add a little milk to make the mix softer if you wish. (Tahine − pronounced 'tar-hinny' − is like peanut butter but made from sesame seeds. It has a milder flavour and creamier texture and is more expensive.)

Storage

Cool, dark, dry storage is your aim. Stake your claim to at least one of the spaces below the sole for your storage. Smile sweetly

but let him see the steel in your eye as you tell of the toothsome delights that will be his if he will only grant you this boon. Areas below water level are the coolest, but bilge stowage must be free from any taint of diesel or damp. Have a good nose around while the skipper is ashore and pick the largest and best space available.

Small plastic mesh baskets such as those sold in Woolworth's are just the thing for stowage of fruit and vegetables. They can be trimmed a little to make them fit the odd shapes that boats have and can be suspended beneath the cabin sole by wedging them between the supports. Avoid using cardboard cartons, no matter how nicely they trim to size. They are not so well ventilated – ventilation is the key to keeping produce fresh – and if from the warmer climates tend to harbour cockroach eggs if not the beasts themselves. Plastic bags are no barrier to cockroaches which can munch straight through, but plastic bins with tight fitting lids, such as ice-cream comes in, are ideal. You'll find the translucent white sort are best for they are made of a longer lasting plastic and you can see the contents.

String hammocks are fine for storage, up to a point. They can swing about if not well fixed, and the skinned fruit comes out with a curious 'hatched' bruising. Beware hammocks with fruit hung in the forward cabin – they are a temptation for the off-watch crew to dip in too easily; you must know the state of the larder at all times. Packets and other soft-pack comestibles stow well in hammocks, however, but not tins; they make a fearful racket banging against the bulkhead and painful missiles if they fall out.

Heavy-duty airtight containers are the answer to most storage problems aboard. Comb all the hardware stores in your area for good quality plastic containers. Don't forget that department stores often carry lines seen nowhere else. I can't pass a hardware store without a quick skitter through to see what plasticware they stock. There is some good stock imported from Spain so if you're that way it's worth looking in some of their ferreterias (hardware stores). I found some excellent tough plastic, wide-mouthed jars which are just the job for cockpit 'nibbles', being watertight and square. Also they did not roll around but stayed put on the sole. Kilner jars can be found, sometimes for pennies, in charity shops and jumble sales. (Look out for stainless steel items here too.) Dawn on *Tacha* (a 39-ft steel Spray) loathes sailing but loves travelling. She cooks complete meals and packs them into Kilner jars. Then, while she's tucked up in her bunk, she knows Eimi is well fed while he sails the boat to the next anchorage.

● Plastic confectionery jars make excellent containers for all sorts of things. Your local sweet shop will usually give them away free, though I know one that asks for a small donation to the RNLI box – no bad thing. They won't take the sort of punishment that the branded items will but are easily replaced.

These sweet bins will hold 6 lbs (approx $2\frac{3}{4}$ kg) of flour and other supplies which can be stowed in hard-to-reach lockers for occasional retrieval. They also make excellent storage for small tools, screwdrivers, pliers and the like, or small bits for the boat such as shackles, thimbles, sail-mending gear, whipping and splicing bits, spare impellers, etc. Torch batteries keep dry and safe in them too. If lockers are damp keep your undies in these transparent screw-topped jars with a scented sachet and you know you've always got a dry pair. Cut in half lengthways they make a good sump drain catch-all – the jars that is. Hang on, this is supposed to be a cook book.

● Have a separate Night-Watch Nosh Box, clearly marked as such, and into it put the night's ration. Day crew should respect this box as sacrosanct for the Night-Watchers – with illicit raiding punishable by keelhauling.

● Label everything. You may know what's in what, but to others it can be a frustrating experience trying to produce a meal in your absence and upsetting all your careful storage with their confused rooting.

With a short cruise in a modern GRP boat there is no real need to de-label and varnish tins, though I do admit to writing the contents and date on the top as an aid to quick sorting and using old stock first.

● Dana and Dee, our sailing gurus, who sailed *The Whistler* (a 46-ft Cal) around the world in ten years and reckoned they rushed it, kept a galley book which noted all the stores in all the lockers. The amount held of each item was shown as a number of dashes (/) and as an item was taken and used they would mark the dash with a back slash so making a cross (X). This gave an instant picture of what had been used and what was left. To save crawling daily into awkward lockers they would 'shop' once a week and keep the current stores handy. When it came time to 'vittal ship' they would consult the galley book to see what was needed. When re-storing they would start with new totals for everything.

● Flour, rice, pasta and pulses are best kept in Tupperware type plastic bins with tight-fitting lids. It goes without saying to buy the freshest stock possible. Flour will keep for a year, though bread comes out best with fresh flour, and you may have to boost self-raising flour with baking powder after it's 'Best By' date. Rice, beans and pulses will keep almost indefinitely if kept dry.

● Biscuits, bread and cakes all need tight-lidded storage. Stout snap lid or screw top plastic containers are the only proof against salty air. Bread will keep for a week in double plastic bags in the dark. Small spots of mould can be trimmed off leaving bread that is still safe to eat, though it tastes better toasted.

Biscuits, for some reason, don't seem to keep for a moment, though seldom through any fault in the storage. Keep the biscuits in their paper wrappers as long as possible; strong-flavoured ones like coconut, ginger and almond will need their own plastic bag if not a separate container if the other biscuits are not to come out tasting the same. If you have bins whose air-tightness you suspect but that are otherwise serviceable try storing the item in a plastic bag within the bin. Seal the bag with a bag tie, or plastic clip such as they give away in supermarkets, or a plastic clothes peg. If the neck of the bag is twisted round, then bent double on itself and caught with an elastic band, it is virtually air/water tight.

● Sugar and salt can be a problem. I keep sugar double wrapped in a screw-topped flare canister. (I couldn't find a recipe I liked for flares so I binned them.) These canisters make excellent storage, and if you don't have an old one you might be lucky to pick one up at a chandlers or boat jumble. They don't come cheap but they really are air/watertight and make good panic bags to keep near the companionway: well labelled to distinguish them from the genuine article, of course. Flare canisters also make good tool containers with rag in the bottom to save the business ends of screwdrivers and the like.

FRESH FOOD STORAGE

White cabbage keeps very well and has a variety of uses. Other green leaf vegetables will keep for a week or so but must be well ventilated or they will smell unbelievably, so eat the leaf first and save the white cabbage for later. The source of smells can be difficult to find on a boat, as Francis Chichester found when he accidentally dropped some vitamin pills in the bilge of *Gypsy Moth IV* on his circumnavigation. It took him ages to locate the origin of the vile smell they gave off as they decomposed.

Yams, parsnips, swedes, carrots and potatoes will keep well in dark, dry, ventilated storage. Onions on a string and garlic keep particularly well and can be tied to a convenient point in the galley. Ventilation is the key to keeping vegetables fresh, plus regular checking to remove the rogues. Washed carrots seem particularly prone to mould.

TIMELY TIPS

● Buy your fruit and vegetables at the last moment but – and this is the important bit – buy if you can from the local market.

There's nothing wrong with supermarket produce except that it's treated to be eaten immediately. It's been washed to within an inch of its life and probably wrapped in plastic. Both these facts guarantee that it will be unfit to eat before the week is out. Fine for the home-cook but no good for the sea-cook. Get your vegetables with good honest dirt on them. Nature made them with a protective coating; wash this off and the rot sets in immediately.

● Most root vegetables will keep for weeks if they are left with a dusting of the earth they grew in. Not piles of earth in the fo'c'sle but the roots piled into an open crate. Inspect them every two to three days and rub out any eyes that are starting on potatoes, otherwise they shrivel and dehydrate. Turn them all over and keep the crate will ventilated, which might involve leaving under-berth lockers partly open. Obvious precautions need to be taken so that stowed items don't come adrift if the going gets rough.

● Chichester wrote in his book *Gypsy Moth Circles the World* that his grapefruit kept for six months, as did lemons. Fruit wrapped in paper seems to keep better, though it is more difficult to examine. The slim moulded trays that separate layers of apples in the supermarket make good separators in lockers, preventing the fruit from touching. They can be cut to shape and will bend to fit the odd contours of lockers.

Cooking Methods

Man took to cooking his food because he discovered heat made some things edible that were not before and others more digestible and tasty, thus increasing the variety of his diet. Baking was probably the first method of cooking, with vegetables pushed into the edges of the fire. He then found that if he separated the food from the fire it was tastier – without the ashes – so he stuck the meat on a skewer and wrapped the vegetable in leaves. Later it occurred to him that if he heated stones the food could be cooked on those, which led him to make a hole in the ground and line it with the hot stones, and the food cooked even better. Then he discovered how to make pots, and the rest is history.

BOILING

Boiling is probably the most basic of cooking methods and there's not a lot I can say about it that you don't already know.

Boiling is safest and vegetables taste best with a minimum of water, which means good pans with tight-fitting lids. Most root vegetables are cooked by boiling.

STEAMING

Leafy vegetables will steam over a pan of boiling potatoes, etc. Pre-cooked rice and pasta can be kept warm or reheated the same way. It is worth getting a steaming pan with holes in the bottom that will fit one of your pans, though a sieve or colander work nearly as well. Rice cooked ahead of time can be reheated in a colander over another boiling pan.

FRYING

This covers eggs whole or as omelettes and Eggy Bread. Cheater's roast potatoes are boiled first then quickly fried to crisp the outside and sprinkled with garlic salt. Burgers, pizza, pan bread and scones also come in the frying group needing a good heavy pan, and with a heavy pan and lid you have a mini-oven. The 'girdle' is a very old method of fatless frying – or open baking – on a hot slab of metal; the modern girdles differ only in having plastic instead of wooden handles.

STIR-FRY

Most vegetables, shredded or chopped small, stir-fry well and this method of cooking is particularly good on boats for the same reason that it was developed in the East. Stir-frying requires the minimum of oil and the shortest cooking time to conserve fuel. The main difference between stir and ordinary frying is the heat level. Ordinary frying is usually done over a medium to low heat, whereas stir-frying is done over a high heat but for a shorter time.

SET ASIDE

Most pastas will cook very well if they are covered with boiling water and then set aside with a tight-fitting lid for 10–15 minutes. They must be stirred occasionally and drained the moment they are 'al dente'. This method releases a burner for other cooking.

PRESSURE COOKING

Almost anything can be cooked in a pressure cooker, and it is one of the sea-cook's best aids. With its locking lid spillage is virtually impossible, and its speed of cooking makes up for its rather bulky stowage problems. (*See* also section on Pressure Cookers in the chapter on Equipment.)

Always cook extra of the evening savoury or base (rice, potato, pasta) to provide a foundation for tomorrow's lunch. That's one less meal to worry about.

BAKING

Baking is filling an enclosed space with hot air in which the food is placed to cook. The oven has developed in many directions since our man with his stones, though this method is still in use among some Pacific Islanders where food, wrapped in leaves, is placed in a hole with hot stones and covered with palm leaves and sand. After several hours the food is cooked to perfection. The Maoris in New Zealand still use this type of oven, called a Hangi.

Ovens – whether heated by solid fuel, gas, electricity or whatever – cook with dry heat. (Microwave ovens cook by 'boiling', so the end results are not quite the same.) Food can be baked uncovered, when the top will probably become browned, which could be a desirable feature, or covered as in a casserole, which is like an oven within an oven. This usually means long slow cooking to render tough food tender and was developed in places where fuel, such as peat, was plentiful.

CASSEROLING

Casseroling can also be done on top of the cooker with the food enclosed in a lidded vessel and left over a low heat for some hours. The advantages of this method are several, not the least that it needs little attention once started and renders practically anything (within reason) tender and edible.

GRILLING

Grilling is a fast method of cooking by searing food under a high heat source. Barbecues are just upside-down grills.

Keeping the residue to a minimum

This is a problem faced by every household but the solution is more complex afloat. Everything these days seems to be wrapped, double-wrapped and then boxed with an outer sleeve, not only in the cause of preserving the contents from damage and spoiling but also as a sales aid.

When stowing goods, try to remove as much of the packaging as possible to leave ashore whilst still guarding its safety. See which items can be decanted into permanent containers or held in plastic bags rather than boxes. Look for cartons instead of tins wherever possible for things like tomatoes, cream, dessert toppings, cooking sauces, etc.

In the food department, cook with minimal residue. Don't peel vegetables unless the skin is inedible (like eddoes and yams). The skins of the more common root vegetables are edible and will go unnoticed if chopped small. Potato skins fry deliciously crisp with Bombay Potatoes see page 109. Besides, peeling vegetables is a bore, so use a stiff vegetable brush to remove dirt and nick out any marked skin. Likewise with fruit: apple and pear skins contain most of the vitamins, and when the fruit is chopped the skins provide colour. Citrus fruit skins are only suitable for a little garnish or jam-making so will have to be kept as garbage – and I wouldn't dare suggest you eat pineapple skins.

But you will find even these small measures will significantly reduce the amount of garbage you have to cart around with you. I don't recommend squashing empty tins flat because of the risk of cutting yourself, especially if you use the kind of tin-opener that leaves the tin with a lethal cutting edge all round. It is worth rinsing the empty tin in the last of the dishwater to reduce the pong later and using it to contain other wet refuse. Empty cartons will pack flat or can be used to hold smelly things and you can fold the top of the carton over to help keep the smell in.

Storing garbage is a problem that faces everyone afloat and highlights the unnecessary expenditure of resources on packaging that is then discarded. Garbage as it accumulates is best kept in several small parcels which are then gathered into larger parcels. Heavy-duty dustbin bags with ties can be stowed in a lazaret when full, to await dumping ashore. Try to keep all refuse as dry as possible; paper kitchen towels used for general mopping up can be stuffed into empty cartons and tins and will soak up the last of any moisture to prevent drips.

EQUIPMENT

It can be enough of a shock to shift from your bright spacious kitchen to the cramped apology of a galley without the added blow of giving up the electric aids that make a non-cook's life tolerable ashore. Don't panic, there are substitutes and compromises and I have searched and found quite a few interesting gadgets. Some have proved themselves so useful that they have earned a place ashore and even replaced their electrical counterpart.

You should be able to find all the following products, with the exception of The Boerner 'V' Slicer, in most good hardware stores.

Food mixers, processors and liquidisers

I'd forgotten what a chore it was to whisk egg whites by hand. Even a rotary whisk seemed hard work. Besides, rotary whisks are usually metal, bulky, need two hands to operate, are difficult to clean and they fight with everything else in the drawer. I found two different designs of pump action whisk made in plastic which can be used with one hand.

The balloon-type whisk, illustrated opposite, came with an egg white separator which holds the yolk without spilling while the whites are whisked. The other design has six little fingers in a circle which curl up at the bottom. These whisks make short work of egg whites and are excellent for other liquid mixing, like omelettes, puddings, batters and drinks. Their simple design is effective, light and easily cleaned and they have proved a boon. My liquidiser seldom sees the light of day now.

You can buy egg separators on their own; I found one, set into a two-size cookie-cutter, and they do make life so much easier. Of course you can do it the old fashioned way by tipping the yolk backwards and forwards between the two half shells but you have to be pretty nifty not to drop any or, worse, snag the yolk. I think the egg separator earns its place. Omelettes are so fluffy if you whisk the whites first before adding the yellows.

The Mouli Julienne and Legume rotary graters by Moulinex make short work of all sorts of grinding jobs, and are very useful for nuts and breadcrumbs as well as vegetables. The plastic

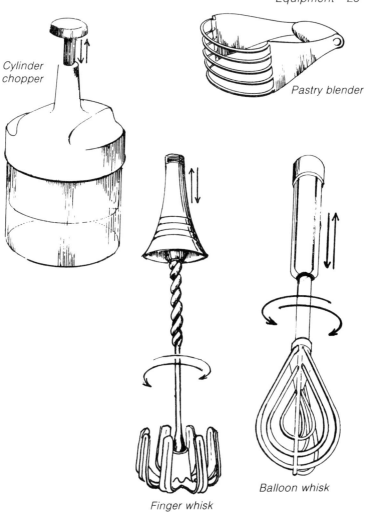

Cylinder chopper

Pastry blender

Finger whisk

Balloon whisk

'V' slicer or 'Jaws'

bodies are easy to clean and the metal parts are rust-proof. The *Julienne* has five discs which grate from very coarse to very fine and will handle all raw vegetables as well as hard cheeses. The *Legume* is for reducing cooked fruit and vegetables to a purée and comes with three grades of sieve inserts. It will also grind nuts, coffee beans and breadcrumbs.

The Boerner Board Chopper is made in West Germany but is known in the UK as 'The Gourmet "V" Slicer'. With it's blade and 'shark's teeth' it is one of my favourite kitchen tools, known affectionately as 'Jaws'. Onions can be reduced to tiny pieces without tears and white cabbage shredded so thin that it would turn the Savoy chef green with envy. Salad vegetables come out as thin as tracing paper and other vegetables and fruit are quickly subdued.

It is shaped like a flat grater but has a 'V'-shaped blade (the earlier model had a single diagonal blade) set in the middle of the frame. Into this you can slide a choice of three inserts which determines the size and shape of the slice. With the fine-toothed insert the 'V' Slicer will produce dainty sticks of most vegetables which look attractive for salads and also cook quickly. With the wider toothed insert one can produce potato chips with the greatest ease. With the third untoothed insert tomatoes and cucumber can be sliced wafer thin and potatoes thin enough to fry for crisps. With the same insert turned the other way, a thicker slice is obtained suitable for hot-pots etc. Vegetables for soup can be prepared in no time and the pieces are so small that peel is no problem.

It is easy to clean with no corners or pockets to trap food but the blades are extremely sharp and I urge caution. Always use the pronged hand grip to hold vegetables except the largest cabbage. Rinse immediately after use and stand it to drain with its teeth to the wall and stow it face down in the drawer with the holder on top – or buy the neat little holder which contains the whole kit.

The difficulty is that the whole package only seems to be available at exhibitions like the International Boat Show and Ideal Home. But it's worth hunting for as I have found it to be one of the most useful gadgets I've ever had; just please observe the safety rules and always use the special handgrip. If you are not likely to go to the above Exhibitions then contact the UK agent, William E. Selkin Ltd, 12 Ludlow Hill Road, West Bridgford, Nottingham NG2 6HF, Tel 0602 232286/7. They supply by post and will accept credit cards.

The cylinder chopper is very efficient and will reduce vegetables, particularly roots and nuts, to small pieces. The pieces are held within the transparent drum so spillage is minimal. But it is noisy and not as versatile as the rotary grinders, though useful for all that.

'Using the fingertips, lightly rub the fat into the flour . . .' so chortles the enthusiast about making pastry. But they don't understand that we *hate* getting our fingers all covered in that sticky mess. For years I refused to make pastry because I detested getting my hands messy. I could guarantee the moment I started, the phone would ring or if we were afloat there would be the clarion call from above. Then I found the **metal pastry blender**. This is a first class little gadget and will crumb the fat into flour as fine and fast as any food mixer. With its fine half hoops it makes short work of cutting in the fat and is easy to clean; pastry holds no horrors for me now. It will also crumb bread.

Though I don't aim to peel vegetables too often, a **swivel peeler** will take wafer-thin slices lengthwise off a carrot that curl attractively and make an interesting difference to salad.

A coarse gauge metal sieve is useful for purées and will even cope with nuts if you break them up first in a plastic bag with a rolling pin and then use the back of a metal spoon to force them through the sieve. But it must be metal and preferably stainless steel.

Pots and pans

Buy the best non-stick saucepans you can fiddle the accounts for; save the cheap stuff for ashore when you have plenty of time and loads of hot water. High quality pans with tight fitting lids will repay you a hundred times by cooking the food faster, more evenly and with less water. They stand up to the hard wear aboard and, if non-stick, are the only sort worth having in my opinion; they make washing up so much easier. After all, if you're being asked to perform miracles you deserve the best equipment, don't you? So go for gold.

A non-stick fry pan is essential as it allows frying with minimal oil. As well as a **heavy skillet** I have found a **dry-fry pan** with a perforated 'mountain' in the middle. The holes let the heat through and the food cooks with only a wisp of fat. But you need a really heavy non-stick pan for sandwiches and pizzas.

One manufacturer, Circulon, has brought out a range of pans with tiny concentric rings on the inside (where they used to be on the outside). Only the top surface of the 'peaks' takes the wear and the 'valleys' remain unscratched. I have two of these pans and they work like a dream. My heavy fry pan, when topped with its lid, is so efficient, I can use it as a mini oven. Pastry and yeast dough can be cooked for a flat flan or pizza by turning it halfway through cooking. You can cook biscuits and scones on it rather like using an old fashioned griddle iron or 'girdle' as it's called in Scotland. The French Le Creuset cast iron cookware now comes with a non-stick surface and although heavy, you could get by with just the fry pan and two saucepans. You would have to improvise a lid for the fry pan as it is not supplied.

A wok (non-stick) is useful for stir-frying. You can stir-fry in a flat-bottomed pan but it does really seem to work best in a wok, something to do with keeping the heat at the bottom and a little oil going a long way.

Since the introduction of the metric system – some of you will have pans in the new sizing, some in the old and some with both, I haven't the faintest idea how much my pans hold; pan sizes to me are Small, Medium, Large or Missionary. So you'll find no pan volumes given in the recipes and will have to judge for yourself which of your pans match my sizing. 'Small' means milk pan-ish, 'Missionary' the sort of thing you'd make jam in.

A steamer is useful for cooking one item on top of another – leaf vegetables will cook over boiling potatoes for instance. It's also good for keeping rice, pasta, etc., hot. You can makeshift with a sieve or colander and a lid over a boiling pan, but the sieve must be metal as I discovered the other day when I ruined a perfectly good nylon one. Actually it was the plastic handle that went; the nylon mesh was fine. The most efficient steamers are made for the job with holes in the bottom of the upper pan and a tight lid but the colander trick works quite well, too. Stainless steel steamers are available as a separate item.

A pressure cooker is one of the vital items in any galley. Some people are nervous of them with the thought of all that pressure inside and because they hiss – sometimes rather loudly. But all pressure cookers are made with a safety valve which will open in the event of the pressure becoming too high, so it is impossible for the thing to explode. I do sympathise with those who are reluctant to use one, but I wouldn't be without mine.

Capacity is a matter of personal preference and stowage space. I prefer the smaller size of about 5 pts (3 litres) because it's easier to handle yet still holds enough for four people. One long handle is preferable to two small ones at the side. I can then hold it to pour with one hand leaving the other hand for balance.

Choose a pressure cooker made of stainless steel; the aluminium ones become pitted after a short time. Besides, the stainless ones look nicer and we're heavily into good gear, aren't we? Tefal do a neat little cooker holding $4\frac{1}{2}$ pts (2.7 litres) which is enough for four people. It has one long handle and a unique locking lid. The pressure release cap does not fall off if you invert the lid (which could be handy in a B2 Knockdown) and the whole thing is easy to clean. Too many gadgets on the lid mean more to get clogged or go wrong.

Care must be taken to see the steam vent is clear of food debris. Always check when cleaning the lid that the valve moves easily and is not blocked with whatever you might have been cooking last.

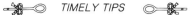 *TIMELY TIPS*

● Liquids will come to the boil again as the pressure is released so remember: release the steam SLOWLY on liquid contents (soups and casseroles) and QUICKLY on solid contents (vegetables, etc.).

● When cooking in a covered dish (*see* the Lentil Loaf or Egg Custard) the dish must be covered to stop the steam mixing with the food. Covers such as foil or greaseproof paper must be secured with string or ties to prevent them from rising and blocking the steam vent in the lid.

● A *heat diffuser*, which looks for all the world like a table tennis bat with holed metal surfaces, is another unlikely but useful item, I have found. You can improvise a small oven from a lid fitting over a baking tin sitting on a heat diffuser. With the heat very low the air in this makeshift oven will become hot enough to reheat pizzas, warm bread rolls or cook a plain egg quiche in a ready-cooked pastry case.

● Depending on the type of fuel used for your cooking there can be difficulties with keeping the heat low. Butane has a horrid habit of blowing out if turned too low. This need not be a serious risk if your cooker has gas-fail protection, but it can be infuriating to find that something you thought was simmering nicely is stone cold. The horror of gas in the bilge if your cooker has no protection is too frightful to contemplate. Constant vigilance is the only answer.

● Paraffin (kerosene) cookers have a problem in that to burn, the oil must be hot enough to vaporise. Hence the need to prime them first with high temperature alcohol. There is a point at which paraffin will not burn any lower without going below its vaporising temperature. Users of paraffin stoves will know how frustrating it is for the flame to go out because it was turned down and they have to go through the whole priming process all over again. Here the heat diffuser, or even two, comes to the rescue. Sadly missed is the now outlawed asbestos mat.

Flasks

Vacuum flasks are useful, especially for the night watch. The late duty cook can leave coffee or soup ready for the taking anytime. A Pump-Pot will dispense the hot liquid without the need to move the pot nor remove its lid – a definite advantage. A wide-mouthed flask will hold bulkier soups and casseroles and can be filled if the barometer drops quickly, suggesting a rough ride ahead. Its contents will be greeted eagerly without further effort later on when life might not be so easy. Individual drinking flasks such as children take to school are invaluable; buy the sort with an inbuilt drinking spout as they are spill-proof even when lying down. These flasks are polystyrene insulated, smash-proof and with their squarish sides won't roll too far when flung down in a hurry. They will keep a drink hot for two to three hours and will fit neatly into the average coaming cuddy. Also handy for the bunk ridden

– voluntary or otherwise – but make sure the liquid isn't too hot initially, as drinking through a spout intensifies the heat.

Yoghurt makers

Making yoghurt is only worthwhile if you are going to be away for more than a week or haven't the space to store lots of the store-bought kind. Making yoghurt is easy, however, and the product is far superior to the commercial sort. If you have a wide-mouthed vacuum flask you can make yoghurt afloat or ashore, and once started it is self-perpetuating. I only make a pint at a time in a litre container to prevent spillage. Ashore one can use an electric yoghurt-maker but I recently found an excellent model that uses no current and comes with its own cheese-maker. The Deva Bridge Yoghurt and Cheese Maker comes as a set or individually. The insulated yoghurt container holds 1 litre, and with its double lid would do duty holding a hot dish at other times. The fine sieve cheese-maker would also do well ashore for making fruit jellies or anything else you might want to strain. A recipe for Simple Yoghurt is given in the chapter on Desserts.

Implements

I admit to being a little paranoid about knives and safety, and in what might seem a contradiction I insist on keeping my cooking knives razor sharp. The dangerous knife is the blunt knife because more pressure is used to cut and that's when the accident happens. With your knives as sharp as a surgeon's scalpel, cutting is made with minimum pressure – the knife does the work – and you'll be so alert that the risk of accidents will be reduced. This is not my homespun philosophy but proven fact. On the lugubrious side, a wound from a sharp knife is cleaner and heals better than a jagged gash from a blunt one, and the latter cuts no less deeply.

Use the right knife for the job. The small paring knife is really only just that. If you are chopping vegetables, particularly roots, use a knife with a long wide blade and let IT do the work. Pressing hard with a small knife to cut a potato can result in disaster when it moves more quickly than you thought it would.

Safe storage for sharp implements is a problem. Loose in a drawer they can catch unwary fingers feeling around. I used to keep mine point down jammed into a deep narrow bin with just the handle tops showing. Even so, they were thrown out and across the saloon in a particularly vicious Mediterranean chop. I now store them edge down in a drawer (with a catch) in cardboard sheaths stuck to the bottom of the drawer or a removable plywood base. The removable base can then be used on a worktop and stowed for safety while under way. I did see one galley where all the knives had their own leather sheaths into which they were replaced immediately after use, even if it meant getting them out again a minute later. This also had the advantage of preserving the edges against abrasion but I'm not sure I could be that disciplined.

A set of rubber spatulas will speed up cleaning as well as getting the last scrap of that precious Chocolate Brandy Mousse (*see* the chapter on Desert Island Desserts). Two is a minimum plus a narrow one for cleaning out measuring cups, spoons and small jars. They will spread fat quickly on a baking tray, pan or tin prior to dusting with flour for biscuits and cakes. (You weren't doing it with your fingers, were you?)

It can be cheaper in terms of resources to wipe a non-stick pan with kitchen paper after scraping with a spatula than using a lot of hot water and washing-up liquid. A pan so prepared can be cleaned with a minimum of water and detergent.

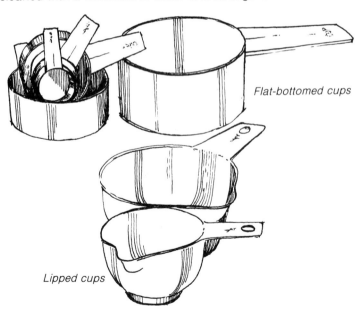

Flat-bottomed cups

Lipped cups

WEIGHTS AND MEASURES

Before we get down to the recipes I'd better explain about the measures used in this book. I never got the hang of imperial measures before being faced with metric. It always seemed to me such a bother having to weigh things, especially fats which messed up the weigh pan. One can give the pan a sly swipe with a cloth after weighing dry stuff but fats or other sticky things means running the hot water and detergent and I get put off. As for liquids, I can never get the level to stop wobbling – and that's on dry land. Or I read off the wrong scale and find, when it's too late that I've mixed litres with pints.

Rescue came when we found ourselves living in the USA and I made the happy discovery that all recipes were given in 'cups' – how sensible: problem solved. A US cup holds 8 ounces of water or half a US pint, compared with our 10 oz half pint. I used to think 10 was the nicer number until, like Saul on the road to Damascus, the realisation hit me with a flash; you can halve 8 three times before it goes to a fraction, 10 only once. Fractions make me fractious. So with all the recipes in this book you will find everything measured by volume in cups or spoons. After all, on a boat, who's going to weigh anything except the anchor. Cup measures are simplicity itself. If you don't want to buy a set of measuring cups then look through your store of mugs and cups and find one that holds 8 fluid ounces of water – one that you don't mind knocking around the kitchen/galley.

With just one such cup you can gauge by eye a half cup, quarter cup, etc., or, if you find yourself on a desert island one day without your measuring cups and before you've had time to sort out some coconut shells, you will find that your two hands, cupped together, will hold the equivalent of 1 cup, if not heaped too high. But it's difficult to fill your hands, when cupped together, without a third hand to help. One hand cupped, will hold $\frac{1}{3}$ of a cup, but it really is so much easier to use measuring cups. They are readily available in hardware stores and cook shops and they have many uses besides measuring.

I have three cup sets (see illustrations opposite and page 39); the stainless steel ones double as mini saucepans for warming small amounts over a very low heat or mug of boiling water. The oldest set were cheap plastic and have lost their handles or developed cracks so I keep them in the flour and rice bins for instant measuring. The third set are flat-bottomed and are used to hold sauces and pickles at table. The best design is gently rounded but flat enough on the bottom to stand on its own. I have also found a mini jug in toughened glass that holds one cup – that's 8 fluid ounces – and is marked in $\frac{1}{2}$ cup, $\frac{1}{3}$ cup and $\frac{1}{4}$ cup.

For smaller amounts *spoon* measures are used, and for practical purposes there is no difference between US, UK or metric spoons. All spoon measures quoted are for *flat/level spoons* – a heaped spoon can carry double a standard level spoon. Fine with the cream in a Pirate's Punch (*see* the chapter on Drinks) but gagging with bicarbonate in a sponge.

The more observant among you will notice that when listing the ingredients I have put the item required *first* and then the amount that's needed, so you can look at a recipe and see at a glance if you've got what it takes, so to speak. I find it very confusing to read the amounts with their metric equivalents as well and then the ingredient. It all gets so jumbled up that I give up nine times out of ten because I can't be bothered to sort it out. After all, this is the information that needs to leap out of the page at you if you're going to be at all interested in taking things further. I hope you agree.

A $1\frac{3}{4}$ pt (1 litre) Pyrex jug is a most useful working container. Use it with the pump whisk to prepare Lemming Surprise Pudding (*see* the chapter on Desserts). Use it as a mortar with a round-ended (handle-less) wooden rolling pin to grind nuts, beans etc. Find a jug that is taller rather than wider as it makes the whisk and pestle more efficient. Another dizzying discovery I made was that very few recipe quantities are mandatory. A bit over or under with the ingredients makes little difference, with the possible exception of liquids. If there's a recipe that you would like to try but are short on quantity for one of the items listed, use your judgement and adjust the rest to suit. Chances are that it will turn out fine. Substitution is another option. If I specify onions and you only have shallots or even just plain old leeks, go ahead, invent a new recipe. For sweetening, I prefer to use runny honey and you will find it in many of the recipes. But if you don't have honey or don't like it, then try granulated sugar, soft brown sugar, muscovado sugar, golden syrup, malt extract or molasses – they get richer tasting (and heavier) in that order. None of the recipes in this book is so sensitive that it can't be abused a little. I've got no time for fine tuning.

Oven temperatures

One doesn't always have the luxury of a temperature control on cookers in boats. Again I have discovered that for most things temperature doesn't matter a whole lot to within 30°F or so; things will either cook quicker or slower. You might have the odd embarrassment, but by and large if in doubt make it cooler than hotter. Things which have taken longer to cook remain more edible than things cooked too quickly – and the cook suffers less trauma (I traumatise easily!).

Recipes are given in Fahrenheit, Centigrade and Gas Mark figures. If, however, your oven is *very* basic, the table below will give you some clues.

Oven	°F	Gas	°C
Warm	300	2	150
Moderate	325–350	3–4	180
Moderately hot	375–400	5–6	190–205
Hot	425	7	220

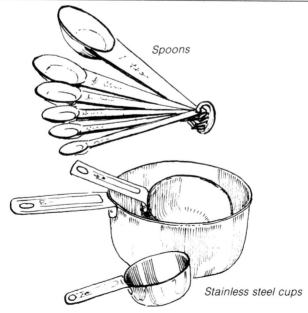

Spoons

Stainless steel cups

SEASONING

Have you ever noticed that when your hostess reluctantly gives you that recipe for the dish you've raved over it doesn't always quite turn out the same way when you do it? Now I'm not saying they're deliberately dishonest but it would seem to me that dedicated cooks have a secretive streak and when passing on a recipe one essential ingredient might just slip their mind. That magic ingredient X is, probably, the seasoning (or one part of it).

The Secret to Success is Seasoning

The trick is so simple it's silly. Why didn't someone tell me before? Well, the answer is, of course, that they've been telling me all along but I didn't take it in. Non-cooks like me, if they do read a recipe in the first place, tend to pass over any bits they don't understand. The recipe says: 'Adjust seasoning to taste.' Adjust? With what, a spanner? Taste? What of?

I never understood seasoning. Salt and pepper I could handle; after that I was in the dark, so rather than get it wrong I'd leave out the seasoning bit. I probably didn't have the right sort anyway. As for tasting what I was cooking, it never occurred to me. It was as if I'd read the words but they didn't filter through.

Wing of bat, leg of toad ...

Taste it and find out what it needs BEFORE it gets to the table so you can correct it, with a bit of luck. I'm going to repeat that for those who weren't listening the first time:

YOU MUST TASTE AS YOU GO ALONG.

And then:

YOU MUST SEASON.

It's probably safe to say that salt was the first seasoning used by man – though more likely by woman. When pepper came on the scene I can't tell you, but the two go together. However, there's more to it than that. Seasoning usually calls for the use of herbs and spices too.

Herbs are the soft parts of fragrant plants, the leaves, stems, flowers and sometimes the seeds and roots are used to flavour food. Most herbs can be grown in the UK; generally the plant dies down annually and puts out fresh soft growth the next season. Herbs can be used fresh but they can also be dried and stored for use throughout the year. Their flavour is usually mild.

Spices come from plants, shrubs and trees growing in hot climates. The berries, seeds, leaves, roots and even the bark are dried and used, sometimes ground. Spices have a more pungent flavour and their addition to food is often dramatic.

Whilst herbs can be grown well in our gentle climate and have been used for centuries in medicines, the pungent spices have a more romantic history, being worth their weight in gold and coming from tantalisingly far away places. There was fierce competition for possession of the Spice Islands and territories; wars were fought to gain the valuable trade and protect the overland routes. Later, when Christopher Columbus sought and found a sea route to India and the Orient it was the seafaring nations who became powerful, plying their trade around the newly discovered Horn of Africa and using the monsoon winds to speed their voyages. It's not too much of an exaggeration to say that the trade in spices played a large part in the development of sailing and navigation.

So what does the term 'seasoning' really mean? Like me, you don't really want to know that spices were originally used to cover the rancid taste of meat that was hardly fit to eat, do you? So shall we just say that 'seasoning' means the addition of herbs and spices to a dish that adds or enhances flavour, colour and eye appeal. Stewed apple is nice, but with a hint of clove it's transformed into something else. It's that 'something else' that we're after. Many a pathetic little mess can be saved by a judicious bit of seasoning.

OK, so there are two problems here:

No. 1 – you've got to analyse what you're tasting.
No. 2 – you've got to work out what to do about it.

 *TIMELY TIP*

● Keep a little wooden spoon for tasting – it saves burning your lips with the stirring spoon.

Fortunately there are short cuts that we can take. If you haven't already got your favourite seasoning I can recommend trying Season-All by Schwartz. Before I had the courage to experiment this was all I used. The trouble was that everything came out tasting the same. It's still very useful for all that, but one should have variety now and then. I was lucky enough to be sent some Crab Seasoning from America and became so enamoured of it that I got too heavy handed and used it on everything bar custard, until my family complained, in tears. It was a bit strong on the chilli, I must admit.

Some claim medicinal properties for herbs but that's not my province, though things like ginger I find very good for seasickness (*see* the chapter on Seasickness), clove oil for toothache and spiced wine makes a lovely comforter for those suffering colds or flu (*see* the chapter on Drinks).

Herbs and spices divide roughly into two sorts, sweet and savoury. However, I did say 'roughly' because quite a few go well on both sides – just don't use them at the same meal. Now our experts, smiling at us from their sunny stainless kitchens, will trill on about popping out into the garden to pick fresh herbs for their dishes. They are the sort who would also have you mill your own flour. Oh, come on now, let's stay in the real world, shall we? Even a dedicated gardener will seldom have more than a dozen herbs growing in the garden, few of them perpetually usable throughout the year.

Dry herbs and spices are excellent and you can have dozens of little jars that need no nurturing. They do need to be kept air-tight, however, and despite making a pretty show on the shelf are better kept in the dark. They also need a little time to develop their flavour once moistened so any that you use as a garnish should be allowed to 'blossom' on the dish before serving. A lot of the spicier seasonings benefit from being added early on and cooked with the onions in oil. Always cook gently and push the seasoning around with the oil to help bring out its full flavour. Most supermarkets stock the big brand names. These brands come packed in small drums or jars with a short description of their uses, and are readily available. Even the ones in glass jars

Grow your own herbs, aboard

are safe on a boat as the glass is very tough, and when empty the jars are useful for storing screws and odd boat bits.

Though by no means exhaustive, the list on pages 49 to 51 gives some of the most popular herbs and spices with suggestions for their use. I have to admit I keep nearly all of them, but the jars are small, and sometimes just looking at them will give me the answer to that daily problem 'what shall we have tonight'.

Date your herb and spice jars with indelible marker so you don't keep them forever. They do eventually loose their zest. A recent shuffle through my assortment revealed a jar dated (by me) '5/83, Ground Cloves', and on opening it smelled just fine, still pungently full of Elizabethan promise after seven years. It must have flown with me from the UK to Cyprus and sailed the length of the Med to sit in Gibraltar for three years before sailing home to Devon, a fair old round trip. Herbs and spices don't go bad but they do eventually loose some of their flavour and strength, so let your nose be your guide.

Other seasonings for your delectation might include proprietary brands that you know your crew like. Don't forget things like

Worcestershire sauce, soy and oyster sauces, Dijon mustard, pickles, chutney, and even, dare I mention it, good old tomato ketchup (*see* Thousand Mud-Flat Dressing in the chapter on Soups). The brand names like Schwartz (part of McCormick) do authentic mixes like Fish Provençal, Sweet & Sour, and Chinese Five Spice that are well worth trying. They also do a range of pepper mixes such as Citrus Pepper with its brightly coloured specks (delicious over Cabbage Cream – *see* the chapter on Vegetables) and Dill Pepper which is really different – lovely in Thick Onion Soup (*see* the chapter on Soups). One of my favourites is mixed peppercorns in a mill giving lots of colourful speckles that make a lovely garnish on light coloured food.

Sharwood's range of oriental curry pastes, chutneys and spices is enormous. Look for their sachet curry mixes, marinades and Indian bread mixes as an aid to quick tasty meals. Never mind if they state it's for meat and you're not cooking meat. I have used them with mixed vegetables and cooked pulses with roaring success. Their Mississippi Marinade, ostensibly for Southern Fried Chicken, works a treat on a fillet of fish. Their Mild Curry Paste is reliably mild and the chutneys richly mellow.

Knorr and Coleman's both make a variety of cooking sauces in cartons and sachets to give you a wide choice of flavours and styles. These products have a long shelf-life of between four and nine months so there should be no storage problems.

Arrowroot is nicer than cornflour for thickening fruit sauces as it stays transparent and is not gluey, but cornflour is good for ordinary thickening. Plain flour, preferably brown, will thicken soups and stews if blended with a little cold water to make a batter but must be well cooked once added to the main liquid. Better still, add it early on at the 'onion' stage and let it cook in the fat at the bottom of the pan before adding the liquid (*see* Instant Lump-Free Sauce in the chapter on Soups).

Creamed coconut is a useful addition to the store cupboard. It looks a little like candle wax but grated or pared with a knife and warmed with a little milk or water makes a delicious cream to add to all sorts of dishes, sweet and savoury. Try adding 2 table-spoons of grated creamed coconut to a curry. Add it to the fool-proof sauce (see page 66) and coat fish fillets. Add it, mixed with a little milk, to yoghurt and sweeten with a little honey for a delectable dip or dessert. You can use it in drinks like hot milk and honey or alcoholic ones like Pina Colada.

Vecon is the trade name of a vegetable paste packaged in dark brown jars and sold in health food stores. Deliciously savoury spread on bread or toast, it also makes an instant warming drink made with 1 teaspoon of the paste mixed well into 1 cup of very hot water. It's useful instead of a bouillon cube in soups and casseroles, and as a drink it is good for the seasick sufferer.

CRUNCHY TOPPING

The results of this five minute exercise will give you a store of crunchy topping that will go well over sweet or savoury dishes and make all the difference to what might otherwise be rather plain fare.

WHAT YOU NEED

Breadcrumbs $\frac{1}{4}$ cup
Buckwheat $\frac{1}{4}$ cup, preferably brown
Mixed nuts 1 tbsp, chopped
Sesame seeds 1 tbsp

WHAT YOU DO

Grill the breadcrumbs under a hot grill in the bottom of the grill pan without the grid or in a shallow baking tin. Stir frequently to prevent burning. Throw in the buckwheat and allow it to toast, then add the mixed chopped nuts and sesame seeds. Keep stirring so that all ingredients get nicely brown. Allow to cool and store in a screw top jar or other air-tight container.

Use it sprinkled over just about anything that needs a bit of 'crunch'. Try it with a little cinnamon and brown sugar on top of a plain yoghurt, Yoghurt Snow (*see* the chapter on Desserts) or ice-cream if you have it. Use it as a garnish on cauliflower cheese or on top of things you don't have the time or inclination to grill, like mashed potato. Add it to muesli, use it as a garnish over cream cheese on crackers, or over Thousand Mud-Flat Dressing on a salad (*see* the chapter on Soups). Even scrambled egg looks 'cared for' with a little Crunch on top. But if you can't even cope with that just bash those crisps again.

Gelatine is a very useful item to have in the kitchen/galley. With it you can make a jelly dessert out of practically any fruit and its juice. Adding it to cheesecake means you don't have to cook the cheesecake. It helps a dessert mousse to set if you haven't a fridge and the weather is warm. You can improvise jellied fruit in a flan by dissolving the granules in the fruit juice, adding honey or jam and pouring over. It helps Summer Pudding to set (*see* the chapter on Desserts) if you haven't a fridge.

Spiced Sugar is just soft brown sugar, light or dark, with a spice (or two) added. This can then be sprinkled on to things that need a little jazzing up. Try Spiced Sugar (with Cinnamon) on a slice of Eggy Bread, or on Banana Bread toasted. If you're frying bananas for dessert sprinkle a little spiced sugar on just before serving. Use Spiced Sugar (with clove) over breakfast cereals for a change or in muesli – it goes well in Miser's Muesli. Spiced Sugar (with Mixed Spice) is nice over fruit salad.

Tomato paste and purée, vegetable purée, garlic purée are useful in tubes. The tomato purée is particularly good because you use only what you want – just a touch or a good squirt – unlike those little tins which you have to use all at once. The garlic purée likewise – it's easier than peeling those little cloves which pop out of your fingers and fall into the bilge. Don't hesitate to use garlic purée whenever a recipe calls for garlic; its so much easier afloat (1 level tsp of purée is equal to 1 clove).

Stock cubes. Where these are mentioned in recipes I would prefer to use vegetable stock cubes, although chicken cubes can be used instead. Beef cubes would not be suitable in most cases, as the strong flavour might fight with the seasoning suggested.

Garnishing is often overlooked by non-cooks yet it can make all the difference to a so-so meal. As a general rule put dark things on light food and light things on dark food. This is nothing new, but it's we cook-o-phobes who need to be reminded to use it. Apart from the obvious ground pepper, try the mixed coloured pepper already mentioned as well as poppy seeds – here a little goes a long way. Pumpkin seeds are a lovely green colour and make an economic replacement for almonds. Strew them over rice salad, muesli or stir-fry. Pound them small and use as a replacement for mixed nuts in cakes. If you've only got the tail end of a wrinkled red pepper, slice it paper thin to strew the strands over cheese on toast; the wrinkles won't show. When grating cheese to top some dish or other, do a little extra and keep it in a small lidded pot – very useful for instant garnish on potatoes, soup, salad, or vegetables and a little goes a long way.   Almost anything green and edible can be used for garnishing savoury food. Don't bother with a knife and chopping board, just take the kitchen scissors and cut the rolled up green stuff directly over the food – much quicker.

You can add a little grated lemon peel to or as a garnish on practically any dish, sweet or savoury. Go on, try it.

Cake decorations like hundreds and thousands and chocolate strands for decorating desserts make all the difference even to a plain yoghurt and a few tubs of whatever your store has to offer will go a long way.

Root ginger is great for all sorts of things, sweet and savoury. Just try adding a little shredded root ginger to stir-fry vegetables.

The root has a smoothish beige skin which you need to remove. I have found if you freeze the root the skin peels off quite easily, otherwise use a peeler. Separate the 'toes' to make peeling easier, then chop or grate into tiny pieces or use a garlic crusher.

It is an essential ingredient in curries, and can make an interesting change to stews and soups (*see* Parsnip and Ginger Soup page 62). Cakes, biscuits, stewed and fresh fruit plus puddings can all benefit from the addition of a little ginger. I wonder if that's where the expression came from, to 'ginger it up'?

Many people, and I am one, believe ginger has medicinal qualities. It has long enjoyed the reputation as an aid to digestion and 'doth give ease to those troubled with gafses of the stomache'.

TO PRESERVE GINGER

WHAT YOU NEED

Root ginger $\frac{1}{2}$ cup
Sugar $\frac{1}{2}$ cup
Water 1 cup

WHAT YOU DO

Simmer all ingredients gently for 15 minutes. Cool and store in screw-top jar. Use for any recipe using ginger sweetened, or try Hot Ginger Posset (*see* the chapter on Drinks), a lovely bedtime alternative to chocolate, and a lot cheaper.

Curry is a blend of herbs, cumin, turmeric, fenugreek and coriander among other things. Most people use a proprietary brand and you may have your favourite. Mine is a mild curry paste by Sharwood because it seems to have a fuller flavour without taking the roof off your mouth. This may be something to do with the fact that it is a thick paste with a certain amount of oil which holds the essences more truly. It comes in a nice sturdy jar, but I still keep it wrapped in a piece of kitchen towel sitting in a plastic bag or it creeps. Used as directed, and cooked with the onion over a gentle heat before adding the other ingredients, the aroma has been known to pull crowds.

Seeds need a mention. Apart from the popular nuts such as almonds, brazils, cashews, dried chestnuts, hazelnuts, peanuts, walnuts, etc., the smaller seeds are useful as garnish or to add interest. Sunflower, sesame, pumpkin and pine kernels are all nice to sprinkle in salads and muesli or to use as a garnish, and the tiny black poppy seeds look good on top of bread rolls, cakes and biscuits. Sprinkle poppy seeds over a salad or add to Thousand Mud-Flat Dressing. Tahine is like peanut butter only made with sesame seeds; more subtle in flavour it is nice in sauces. Peanut butter is useful, not just to spread on bread but to make a delicious savoury sauce (*see* the chapter on Soups). Commercial peanut butter tends to have added sugar but you can get it without, or make your own, though I think that's going a bit far on a boat. Cashew nut cream is heavenly and priced at about the same height; you may find it in a health food store and it could be sanctioned as an occasional treat, adults only.

Incidently, I do hate that term health food store but can think of no alternative. Whole food store sounds a bit way out conjuring up pictures of sandals, fringed skirts and long hair. There is no doubt that interest is increasing in food which has not been processed beyond recognition with all sorts of additives we may not want. But you don't want to spend all your free time husking wheat or grinding your own corn when you can buy it ready done; there's a middle line somewhere.

Oriental stores, sometimes called 'Ethnic' can be a mine of intriguing new things to cook. My local one is always busy, but the staff are friendly and will willingly explain how to cook something I'm not sure about. Many oriental foodstuffs are dried and will keep without refrigeration, and I have found it worth exploring and experimenting to see what the crew like and what will translate to the galley.

MARINADES

Marinading is a well-known method of preserving food (mainly meat) and the Chinese were using it to perfection centuries ago. Basically a marinade is a libation of ingredients that will retard spoiling and increase the tenderness and flavour of the dunked item.

GENERAL MARINADE

Combine $\frac{1}{2}$ cup wine (any old stuff except for his old Premier Cru that is), $\frac{1}{2}$ cup wine vinegar and 1 tablespoon oil (preferably olive) with 1 clove of crushed garlic or 1 teaspoon of puree/granules, 1 teaspoon of Herbes de Provence, 1 teaspoon of freshly ground pepper, 1 teaspoon of honey.

Use this marinade for chopped fresh vegetables. Allow them to soak for about 1–2 hours before draining and cooking. Discard any remaining marinade after use.

MARINADE FOR FISH

To the basic marinade given above add 1 teaspoon tarragon and a dash of Worcestershire sauce. Try adding ginger for oily fish and experiment with other spices.

WHAT TO DO

This simple marinade will render a fish fillet into a gourmet's delight. Pour the liquid over the fillet then turn it over so it is well coated. Cover the dish and leave in a cool place for 2 hours. You can go on like this all day and cook the fish in the evening or keep it until the next day without refrigeration. Most fillets will be nicely marinated in 4–6 hours. Discard any remaining marinade after use.

POPULAR HERBS AND SPICES

Name	Suggested uses
Allspice	Puddings, cakes, fruit pies, some vegetables, try on squash.
Basil	Tomatoes, squash and pasta.
Bayleaf (ground)	Pickling, soups, sauces, vegetables.
Cardamom	Fruit salad, muesli, fancy pastries, fruit cup.
Cayenne pepper	Just about everything (except custard) but particularly seafood and chowders, cheese dips, eggs, pasta.
Celery salt	Seasoning for most savouries.
Chilli mix	Chilli Con Carne, curry, and (sparingly) sweet and sour sauce, dips, soups and stews.

Chinese Five Spice	Stir fries, vegetable dishes.
Cinnamon	Cooked and raw fruit, hot drinks, buns, cakes, sweet sauces, pumpkin pie, yams.
Pepper mixes	Soups and stews, sauces and dips, individual seasoning and garnish.
Cloves	Apple pie, puddings, cakes, pickling, hot posset (a hot drink made with wine/ale and the addition of herbs and spices to ward off the ague, today's mulled wine).
Coriander	Apple pie, biscuits, pickling.
Cumin	Curry, chilli, rice and lentils.
Dill weed/seed	Pasta, seafood, vegetables (especially tomatoes), potato salad, curry, rice salad and garnish.
Garlic powder, granules, puree, salt	Use it in just about everthing except custard (OK, go ahead, try it).
Garam Masala	Curry, lentils, rice salad.
Ginger, ground or preserved	Cakes, fruit, drinks, pickles, vegetables, soup.
Herbes de Provençe	Soups, casseroles – a traditional mix of herbs that can bring the Mediterranean to your galley.
Italian mix	Authentic mix for pasta.
Lemon grass	Marinades, rice, fish sauces, tisane.
Mace	Like nutmeg, as a garnish, desserts, cakes.

Marjoram	Soups, vegetables, fish sauces.
Meat tenderiser	Good antidote for jelly fish stings – seriously (*see* the chapter on Miscellaneous).
Mint	Rice salad, taboulé, with sugar for peppermint.
Mustard	Pickles, eggs, cheese, sauces, dips.
Nutmeg	Puddings, cakes, custards (*trust* me), vegetables.
Oregano	Pasta sauces, vegetables, soups, pizza, chilli.
Parsley	Soups, salads, garnish.
Paprika	Mild – use as garnish over light coloured food or when you can't be bothered to brown under grill.
Rosemary	Traditionally for savouries but try in spiced buns.
Sage	Beanburgers, cheese dips, soup, vegetable stews.
Season All	Branded Mix – good for when you can't think (except in custard).
Tarragon	Tomatoes, mushrooms, marinades, onion soup.
Thyme	Garnish on tomato salad, soups, vegetable stews.
Turmeric	Adds yellow colour to rice and curries, egg salad.

IN THE GALLEY

Train your crew to eat with a fork for most dishes (though you can allow them a spoon for soup). Eating with a fork in the American fashion makes sense; it also makes less washing up.

Whether you use paper, plastic, melamine or china plates is up to you. Paper plates on passage save time; they are also biodegradable. Wandering around a pine and cane furniture shop some time ago, I came across some woven cane paper plate holders (made in Taiwan). These support a 9″ (23 cm) paper or plastic plate and stop it folding up prematurely, dropping its contents into your lap or even, with luck, into someone else's. Try a camping shop.

If you haven't got a cover for the sink and can't get someone to make you a wooden one, try looking for a metal tray whose lip will overhang the edge of the sink. This gives you another working surface and anything spilt stays within the confines of the tray. A round tray will work in a square sink as long as it's supported on all four sides. Square trays in round sinks don't work so well. Best is 'square in square' and 'round in round'. To stop the tray vibrating in sympathy with the engine, as it surely will, slice a wine cork in $\frac{1}{4}$″ (6 mm) slices and stick them under the rim of the tray with epoxy glue. This also allows some ventilation to the sink. The tray is also a great way to hide washing up.

Nowhere to stack the wet dishes? Suspend a plastic colander by three lengths of light braided line to the under part of the side deck which, if you are lucky will be over the sink. This will take an amazing number of items where they will quickly dry while you do something more interesting. If the lines aren't too long it will swing happily even when full in a seaway. You may want to put a little tail on one side to hook it out of the way while working or when the going really gets rough.

A round bread board with a 'gulley' around the edge is useful when cutting up citrus fruit. The juice will fall into the gulley and can then be poured off into the dish using a broad bladed knife as a spatula to squeegee the last drops off. If you're really keen you can carve out a small 'V' shaped pouring lip at one point.

With regard to chopping boards, regardless of the material from which they are made, mark the side you use for onions and keep the other side for the sweet things.

A thermos held in a string bag hooked just inside the main hatch is a good way for the Night-Watch to have their coffee. If the bag is secured at the bottom as well so it doesn't swing about, then the flask can be retrieved easily by those in the cockpit. String bags are ideal because you can see what's in them and they can be tied at the bottom through one of the many holes.

If you have a standard two burner top to your cooker with a fiddle rail all round the outside, consider having a stainless steel tray made, measuring the full depth of the cooker but about half the full width. Have a generous lip along the narrow ends and make the tray about $1\frac{1}{2}''$ (4 cm) deep or enough to clear the burner below it. As the whole cooker is gimballed the tray swings with it and you can make drinks safely while going hard to windward in a nasty little chop – I know, I've done it. Again, anything spilt remains in the tray and can be surreptitiously tipped back into the mug. Alternatively line up mugs in the sink when pouring.

Whereas the measurement of the tray, front to back, is defined by the fiddle rail, the width dimension is something to think about. Check the size of the bottom of your pans and kettle; you'll want to stand them in the tray. Though plastic and paper plates should not be put on the tray if it's hot, it will warm china ones very well and you can serve and leave the plates covered if an emergency, like the distress call of a creature with an empty glass, temporarily demands your attention.

If you can't find a stainless steel factor or the exchequer doesn't allow it, look for square-sided roasting pans. They won't be stainless steel but they are cheap and easily replaced. Another possibility is to use a photographer's dark-room pan as they are made in stainless steel as well as the more usual plastic; you'll find the names of suppliers in most of the photographic magazines, or try the *Yellow Pages*. It's worth pursuing – this tray is one of the most useful gadgets in the galley.

Blue Peter fans will be pleased to know that the heyday of the empty washing-up liquid bottle and sticky backed plastic is not gone. Actually the WULB is a bit narrow and better service is gained from that 'thick bleach' bottle which is larger, of stronger plastic and is also a nice blue to match the boat. These and similar, when you behead them at shoulder level, make good bins for holding cutlery. Stack the knives and forks business end down and the spoons up. This way you'll see at a glance which is which and be free from attack by the sharp bits. They can be wedged side by side in a top opening locker.

Jumbo containers of squash or milk can be modified to make useful bins by cutting out the shoulder opposite the handle, with a bit of luck this will remove the stopper as well. They can be wedged into lockers and will hold any kitchen hardware and bits and pieces. You might care to pass this tip on to the skipper who can use them to store cans and tins that will rust and leave marks and otherwise roll around the lazaret. Don't let him pinch yours – make him get his own containers. Engine oil and bilge cleaner come in the size he'll need.

Plastic string bags for shopping are a must. No boxes – there can be bugs in boxes. String bags hold amazing amounts, stow in a pocket, locker or hang up. But some might consider their most vital function is as a wine cooler. A bottle of wine, swathed in a tea towel inside a string bag, suspended over the stern by a strong line will keep nicely cool if you have no fridge or no room in it. If the going is reasonable or you are already snugly anchored hang the saturated article from the back-stay. If under way take a tie from the bottom of the bag as well, to stop the precious item smashing itself. The day's cellarman should keep the cloth well soaked and the wind will do the rest. You could even make a suitable holder as I did using heavy cloth (a piece of old woollen blanket is good) with ties sewn in top and bottom. Yacht acrylic, though smarter, is no good as it dries too quickly.

Rake through jumble sales, charity shops and government surplus stores. These are a mine of goodies especially for ex-mess stainless steel utensils which have an honest battered air about them. Charity shops very often have a slightly more upmarket line in stainless steel items, unwanted presents, etc.

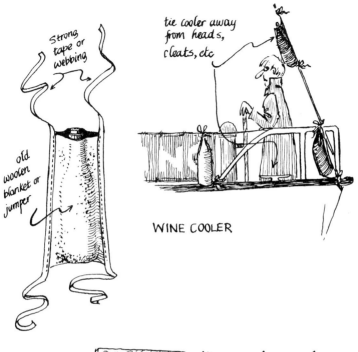

Strong tape or webbing

tie cooler away from heads, cleats, etc

old woolen blanket or jumper

WINE COOLER

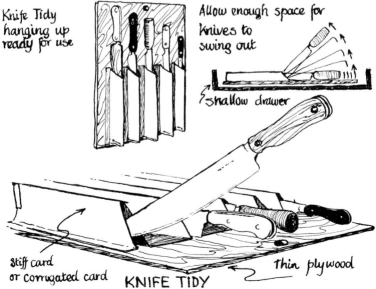

Knife Tidy hanging up ready for use

Allow enough space for knives to swing out

shallow drawer

stiff card or corrugated card

Thin plywood

KNIFE TIDY

In the ordinary way I think plastic table cloths are pretty naff but they have their uses afloat. Firstly, there is thick plastic cloth which is fabric backed and comes on a long roll 60″ (1.5 m) wide. One of the major department store groups stocks an attractive range of this material with the same patterns as their own furnishing fabrics. One yd (1 m) metre square of this heavy-duty fabric on the saloon table will allow you a decent size work top. With the cloth well secured using drawing-board clips you can roll pastry and knead bread and at the end of the session the debris can be gathered up and shaken over the side (out of site of land, of course).

There is also a lightweight plastic 'lace doily' (don't wince) type of cloth, supplied on a roll about 14″ (35 cm) wide. This makes a good non-stick surface for trays or the saloon table and doesn't seem to stain so readily as the thicker foam pads sold for the same purpose. It's a lot cheaper too. Besides, why shouldn't we have a little daintiness about what is otherwise a rather spartan environment. I'm sure you can quell any threatened revolt with a glance.

Salt Water in the Galley

IF you're sure of that lovely crystal-clear blue water, do by all means use it for cooking. But not straight – it's much too salty. Try a 1:1 mix first and adjust as you think fit. It's fine for scrubbing vegetables and dish washing (with a final rinse in fresh water).

SOUPS, SAUCES, STARTERS AND SNACKS

Soups

Soup should have a theme or it's always the same. As soup can form a large part of your repertoire for longer passages when the night-watch want something more than tea and biscuits, you need variety to stave off boredom. Luckily, soup is one of the easiest things to invent and improve, but first take your theme.

By 'theme' I mean decide what the major flavour is to be and then add only ingredients that will enhance rather than fight it. For instance, if you decide that tomato is the theme for today, don't add carrot as the two don't go well together. Surprisingly though, if you make a carrot soup, just a little tomato paste gives a nice bite.

Soup consistency can be anything from a clear consommé to a broth so thick you could trot a mouse across it. Really thick soups can be a main meal with lots of wholemeal bread. Soup is also a good way to get liquids into the system, as sailing can be dehydrating, contrary to opinion. A light soup is an excellent way to welcome back your sea legs and there's nothing that revives quite like a good hearty soup when you've thrashed your way up wind with a foul tide or waited for it's return to release you from an unscheduled stop-over on a rogue sand bar.

Barley is a useful addition in soups to thicken – try barley flakes which cook in 10 minutes, much quicker than whole barley. Try instant potato for thickening as well as the more usual cornflour and wheat flour. Farina is potato flour and will thicken soups and stews; mix it with a little cold liquid first.

Even the humblest ingredients can make a good soup. If you're standing off till daybreak before making that final landfall and the larder is bare except for a couple of onions, you can lash up a soup that will be talked about for seasons to come.

THICK ONION SOUP

This is a quick, tasty soup and the chunks of sweet onion, if not overcooked, crunch nicely. Serve with hot Onion Bread (see page 147) then breathe on the sails for that extra $\frac{1}{2}$ knot.

WHAT YOU NEED
(per person)

Onions   1 large
Garlic $\frac{1}{2}$ clove or as much as you like
Fat $\frac{1}{2}$ tbsp (butter, margarine or oil, in that order of preference)
Brown flour   1 rounded tsp
Cheese   Just enough to grate over the top of each serving
Stock   1 cup water with $\frac{1}{2}$ stock cube
Seasoning
Ground bayleaf
Herbes de Provence   1 pinch

WHAT YOU DO

Chop half the onions very small using 'Jaws' (*see* p. 30); chop the other half in large pieces, 1″ (25 mm) square. Peel and chop the garlic and cook with the seasoning and small pieces of onion very gently in the fat without browning. Sprinkle in the flour and blend well with the onion allowing a minute or two for it to cook. Slowly add the stock and bring to a gentle simmer, stirring until the soup thickens. Add the large onion chunks and simmer till they are just done, i.e. tender and transparent but still crisp. Taste and add a little salt if required. Grate some cheese over each serving or top with crumbed potato crisps or both.

TIMELY TIPS

● The secret of this soup is not to overcook the big chunks of onion, which lose their sharp bite when cooked gently and become delightfully sweet.

★ *VARIATIONS* ★

★ Add a good slurp of sherry and call it Thick Spanish Soup; with white wine it's Thick French, vodka Thick Russian and so on.

★ Being fresh out of cheese one day I surreptitiously grated the rind from the last of the Christmas Stilton over the soup. The evidence melted obligingly but the flavour was an unmistakeable hit.

★ Throw in $\frac{1}{4}$ cup red lentils per person with the finely chopped onion and cook until lentils are half done (about 5–7 minutes) before adding the larger chunks of onion for the final simmer. This recipe can be the base for practically any hot and hearty soup and you can add nearly anything you have left over. Just remember not to add the large pieces of onion until the last five minutes of cooking so they remain crunchy.

★ Try finely chopped vegetables, small pieces of ham and sweetcorn kernels or mushrooms whole if they're tiny or chopped small if larger.

★ One slice of bacon, grilled crisp and cut into fragments gives a nice flavour; it's amazing how far one slice can be made to stretch.

★ When the soup is just about cooked, stir it vigorously to make a whirlpool and carefully drop a raw egg into the centre. Simmer until the egg is poached. This is a complete meal; excellent for frail sailing tummies.

SAHIB'S SOUP

This soup is a good one for using up leftover rice, and the hint of curry makes a satisfying dish if served with plenty of your own brown bread. It's a sort of Mulligatawny.

WHAT YOU NEED
(for 4)

Butter   2 tbsp (butter is best but other fat will do)
Onions   1 large, finely chopped
Celery   1 stalk, chopped as fine as possible
Carrot   1 large or 2 medium, grated
Flour   3 tbsp, brown preferably
Stock   4 cups water with chicken or vegetable cube
Rice   1 cup cooked, more or less, depending on what
you have left over
Seasoning
Curry paste   1 tsp (you can add more if you wish)
Bayleaf   1 leaf or $\frac{1}{2}$ tsp ground bayleaf

WHAT YOU DO

In a heavy saucepan, melt the fat and gently fry the onion without letting it brown. Add the curry paste, stir, then add the celery and carrot, stirring all the time. Add the bayleaf in either form. Sprinkle on the flour, stirring to mix well with the vegetables and allow to cook for a few minutes. Slowly add the stock, stirring to thicken the broth and allow to brew a little longer, then add the rice and simmer just long enough to heat through. Taste it to see if it needs some salt as curry pastes vary in their content. Fish out the bayleaf (if used whole) before serving.

★ *VARIATIONS* ★

★ If there's a chicken carcass to hand you can add the last few shreds of meat or throw in the carcass during cooking to add flavour but be sure to fish it all out before serving.

★ Add a drop or two of port or sherry – go on, be a devil, it does make a lovely rich soup.

JOHN'S SKYE SOUP

Serve this one hot or cold with a twirl of cream and a garnish of chopped parsley and garlic croutons (from a packet).

WHAT YOU NEED
(for 4–6)

Long-life orange juice 1 carton
Long-life creamed tomatoes 1 carton
Seasoning
Salt
Pepper

WHAT YOU DO

Simply tip equal quantities of the fresh orange juice and creamed tomatoes into a pan and heat gently. Taste and add a little salt, tasting again, then add some ground pepper. Serve without allowing the soup to boil, and drizzle a little cream or yoghurt in the centre of each portion.

★ *VARIATIONS* ★

★ You can serve this soup cold – it's sensational on a very hot day.
★ Try oregano as an additional seasoning, or basil.

FIVE MINUTE SOUP

In a hurry, can't be bothered or there's nothing ready and they're all screaming for food? Try this one: 3 minutes preparation and 2 minutes to cook – in the pressure cooker.

WHAT YOU NEED
(for 4)

Stock 4 cups of water with 2 vegetable stock cubes
Butter 2 tbsp
Onion 1 large or 2 small, chopped fine
Carrot 1 large or 2 small, grated or chopped fine
Flour 2 tbsp of plain brown or anything else
Lentils $\frac{1}{4}$ cup

WHAT YOU DO

Put the kettle on to boil 4 cups of water. Melt the butter in the pressure cooker, throw in the onions and carrots and stir. Open both stock cubes and chop into small pieces, toss into pan and stir till it begins to bubble. Add in the flour and mix it well till it sizzles. Pour on a little of the boiling water, mix with the flour and vegetables, then gradually add the rest of the water and the lentils, stirring to make sure everything is mixed well. Close the lid on the pressure cooker and bring to full pressure (which shouldn't take too long) and time it for 2 minutes.

During these 2 minutes you've just got time to make sandwiches or provide crackers and cheese.

★ *VARIATIONS* ★

★ Most root vegetables can be substituted for the carrot, grated or finely chopped.

★ If using stronger tasting vegetables like parsnip or swede and there's some beer around, use some in the stock.

PARSNIP AND GINGER SOUP

A bowl of this soup looks quite unpretentious but the first sip usually draws nods of approval.

WHAT YOU NEED
(for 4)

Butter 2 tbsp
Flour 2 tbsp, brown preferably
Stock 3 cups water with 1½ vegetable cubes
Parsnips 2 cups grated (young parsnips are best)
Seasoning
Garlic 1 clove, crushed or 1 tsp purée/granules
Ginger 1″ (25 mm) root or 1 tsp dried
Herb pepper 1 tsp

WHAT YOU DO

Melt the butter in a heavy pan, throw in the seasoning and push it around. Add the flour and when it has warmed, mix with the butter, letting it sizzle for a while without browning. Add ½ cup of stock and blend till thickened and then add the rest of the stock. Toss in the grated parsnip, cover and simmer gently until parsnip is soft. Pass the lot through a coarse sieve before serving.

CELERY AND LENTIL SOUP

A modest little soup this but easy to make, and if the celery is not quite smart enough to be seen raw it will do well enough as soup.

WHAT YOU NEED
(for 2)

Stock 2 cups water with 1 cube (vegetable or chicken)
Garlic 1 clove or $\frac{1}{2}$ tsp granules/salt
Lentils $\frac{2}{3}$ cup
Celery 2 stalks, chopped small
Seasoning
Garam Masala $\frac{1}{2}$ tsp

WHAT YOU DO

Make up the stock, adding the garlic and Garam Masala. Heat to boil then turn down to simmer. Add the lentils and leave to cook while you chop the celery very small. Add the celery immediately and allow everything to simmer gently until the lentils are cooked. Push the whole lot through a coarse sieve or blender if you can. If not, serve as is with a drizzle of cream, yoghurt or a few strands of grated cheese and some chopped parsley.

★ *VARIATION* ★

★ This works with celeriac also.

SPICY COCONUT SOUP

Serve this delicately flavoured soup and transport yourself and crew to a Pacific Paradise.

WHAT YOU NEED
(for 4)

Onion 1 thinly sliced in rings
Oil 2 tbsp
Lemon peel Some thin strips
Stock 3 cups water with 1 vegetable cube
Lemon juice Squeeze 1 whole lemon
Prawns $\frac{1}{2}$ cup, cooked, tinned or fresh
Bean sprouts 1 cup
Creamed coconut 1 cup, crumbled (*Ingredients cont.*)

Seasoning
Curry paste 2 tbsp (try Sharwood's Thai Hot for authenticity)
Fresh chilli pepper 2 tbsp thinly sliced (optional)

WHAT YOU DO

Fry the onion gently in the oil, add the curry paste, lemon peel and stir to combine. Add the stock and bring gently to the boil, cover and simmer for 5 minutes. Add the lemon juice, prawns, sprouts and crumbled coconut and allow to simmer for 10 minutes until the coconut has dissolved. Serve garnished with some desiccated coconut, if you have it, or flaked almonds. For extra pungency add the chilli pepper.

POTATO AND LEEK SOUP

A good old-fashioned English soup, this. They serve it cold in France and call it Vichyssoise, but that needn't worry us here.

WHAT YOU NEED
(per person)

Leek 1 small
Potato 1 medium
Butter $\frac{1}{4}$ tbsp
Stock 1 cup water with 1 cube (vegetable or chicken)
Cream 1 tbsp
Arrowroot 1 tsp (optional)
Seasoning
Celery salt to taste, parsley or anything else green chopped for garnish

WHAT YOU DO

Chop the leeks small (include some of the tender inner green leaves) and soak them in salt water while you clean *but don't peel* the potatoes. Chop these small using the 'Jaws' or a sharp knife or grater. Melt the butter in a heavy pan and gently sauté the drained leeks and potatoes, taking care not to brown. Add the stock and simmer until the potatoes are soft. Push through a coarse sieve, Moulinex Legume or use a masher. Add the cream and seasoning and then taste. Add a little salt if it seems too bland. You can also thicken with a little arrowroot if desired.

★ *VARIATIONS* ★

★ 1 small pot/tin/carton of double cream does for 4–6 people, or 2 if you're greedy.

★ This is another soup that can be jazzed up with a drop of white wine, though I think it's best straight.

★ If you're out of cream, use yoghurt, cream cheese or fromage frais; different but still nice.

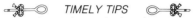 *TIMELY TIPS*

● Any leeks that won't go through the sieve, turn back into the pan. If you're ashore, put the whole lot through the blender.

WANTON SOUP WITH GINGER DUMPLINGS

This is really a mock Chinese Wuntun soup that looks and tastes exotic. A clear broth with tiny spicy dumplings, it's surprisingly easy to make – but you don't tell them that.

WHAT YOU NEED
(per person)

Green leaf vegetable $\frac{1}{4}$ cup chopped (this can be anything – cabbage, spinach, spring greens, etc.)
Brown flour (SR) 2 tbsp
Suet (beef/vegetable) 1 tbsp, grated
Stock 1 cup water with $\frac{1}{2}$ vegetable cube
Mushrooms 1 small, fresh, sliced thin
Seasoning
Oregano, powdered ginger 1 pinch of each per person
Salt 1 tiny pinch per person

WHAT YOU DO

Wash and chop the green leaves very small, but cut some long thin strands for variety. Mix the flour, suet and seasoning with just sufficient cold water to make a dry dough. Form into small balls the size of a marble and toss in flour to stop them sticking together. Heat the stock and taste; add a little salt and pepper if it seems bland. Add the dumplings and the green leaves and cover the pan. Simmer gently until the dumplings have swollen to twice their size. Add the sliced mushrooms and serve immediately.

TIMELY TIPS

● This is a quick soup – with the leaves cut so small they cook in the same time as the dumplings and should look bright green.
● To test the dumplings for doneness, break one open; it should look dry and fluffy inside.
● Mushrooms need hardly more than heating through.
● You can substitute $\frac{1}{2}$ tablespoon of dried mushrooms if fresh are unavailable. Start them off first in the stock to give them time to rehydrate or, if all else fails, use tinned.

Hot Savoury Sauces

UNBELIEVABLE WHITE SAUCE

Remember when the Domestic Science teacher would stand looking over your shoulder for ages while you carefully stirred the roux to avoid lumps? Then, just when you thought it was safe, you'd find those nasty little hard bits and no gold star for you that week. If you want to know a quick, easy and GUARANTEED Foolproof Lump-Free way of making a white sauce then follow me.

WHAT YOU NEED
(for 2)

Fat 2 tbsp
Flour $\frac{1}{4}$ cup (preferably brown or mixed)
Milk 1 cup

WHAT YOU DO

On the bottom of the pan put the fat on one side and the flour on the other and leave them separate. Warm over a medium heat and when fat melts blend it with the, now hot, flour. Turn up the heat a little and spread the mix around the pan and leave it to cook till it sizzles. Don't stir it. This will take about 3–4 minutes all told. The important thing is to let the flour cook well without browning; it will sizzle and look lighter in colour if you are using brown flour.

When the flour mix is well cooked, pour in $\frac{1}{4}-\frac{1}{3}$ cup of milk and DO NOTHING ELSE. Don't touch it or stir it – don't even bother to look at it until you see the milk starting to rise to the boil. Let it really froth well, then stir like fury (you may have to pull the pan off the heat momentarily). The mix will blend without lumps and come away clean from the sides of the pan. Return the pan to the heat and pour in a little more milk to heat. Wait till it starts to come to the boil again and then stir, though not so vigorously or it will slop over the top. Now you can go on adding liquid, wine, etc., to get the consistency you want, plus other ingredients.

All this takes much longer to tell than to do. It may sound complicated but give it a try and be amazed. This method also releases you from standing stirring endlessly, another bonus.

If you haven't tried brown flour, give it a go. Sauces made with brown flour or a mix of brown and white have a lovely golden colour with little specks of bran. White sauce looks so anaemic by comparison. The other advantage is if you should burn anything the bits won't show so much.

★ *VARIATIONS* ★

★ Once you have the basic white, or in this case golden, sauce you can add what flavours you like.

★ Try cheese. It doesn't matter how roughly you chop the cheese because it will melt, so don't dirty the grater. Cheddar is perfect on its own but milder cheeses do need a little help with seasoning, like Season-All or celery salt or garlic salt. The last scrapings of a Stilton – I've already admitted to using the rind – or other strong cheese makes a tangy sauce to go with crunchy vegetables like calibrese, cauliflower, purple sprouting broccoli or sprouts.

★ A sprinkle of ground cumin gives a delicate curry flavour or you can go the whole hog and use a little curry paste. This is a nice sauce over hard boiled eggs – hot or cold – on a rice nest and you can make the curry as hot or as mild as you like.

★ Use the vegetable water or a mix of half and half with the milk to make the sauce.

PEANUT BUTTER SAUCE

This is a lovely coating sauce to use with noodles or spaghetti. With the peanut butter to give the protein, a bowl of pasta with this sauce can be a complete meal, with a salad.

WHAT YOU NEED
(for 4)

Peanut butter $\frac{1}{4}$ cup (crunchy is best)
Oil   3 tbsp
Garlic   1 clove, crushed or tsp of garlic
powder/granules/paste
Seasoning
Soy sauce   1 tbsp
Garam Masala   1 tsp
Garnish   Chopped parsley/chives/celery leaves

WHAT YOU DO

Gently warm the peanut butter, oil and garlic, stirring to form a smooth paste. Add the seasoning and thin with a little water, milk or cream if you want a more flowing sauce.

Coat hot cooked noodles or pasta with the mixture, turning with a spoon to make sure it goes all round. Garnish with chopped parsley or chives.

★ *VARIATIONS* ★

★ You can use dried chives, but soak them in a small quantity of hot water while you make the sauce to give them a chance to swell. Do the same with dill weed.

★ If you don't have any soy sauce try Worcestershire sauce instead – but only a few drops as it's pretty strong stuff.

SHRIMP SAUCE

This is a light sweet and sour sauce which goes beautifully with shrimps or prawns. Serve it, with the shrimps/prawns, with crisp stir-fried vegetables and fluffy rice for a quick imitation of a traditional Chinese dish.

WHAT YOU NEED
(for 2)

Arrowroot $\frac{1}{2}$ tbsp
Water 1 cup
Corn syrup $\frac{1}{4}$ cup (or maple syrup)
Tomato paste 1 tbsp
Vinegar 1 tbsp

WHAT YOU DO

Mix the arrowroot with a little of the water till blended, then add the other ingredients and mix well over a gentle heat till thickened. Pour over shrimps or prawns.

Cold Savoury Sauces

THOUSAND MUD-FLAT DRESSING

This is a good quick sauce for any cold shellfish dish or tuna salad or avocado; finger-licking good in sandwiches and pitta pockets to moisten the contents.

WHAT YOU NEED

Salad cream The '57' variety, nothing fancy
Tomato ketchup That much maligned favourite of the
all-night café
Milk (optional)
Seasoning
Garlic A good dash of granules or powder

WHAT YOU DO

Simply mix the salad cream and tomato ketchup 2:1 proportions and thin with a little milk if required. Add the seasoning and mix well before pouring over the shellfish, tuna or salad. Do not thin for sandwiches and pitta pockets. Garnish with a sprinkle of something dark: chopped parsley, ground pepper, fine strands of fresh sweet pepper, paprika or chives. (Dried chives can be revived by soaking in a little hot water in a measuring cup for a few minutes before draining on kitchen paper and sprinkled.) You can adjust the proportions of salad cream and tomato ketchup either way as desired.

★ *VARIATIONS* ★

Seasoning: garlic is the best, in my opinion, closely followed by ginger. But you might care to ring the changes:

★ Ground bay leaf, chilli seasoning mix, dill weed, dill seeds, cayenne pepper, celery (salt/flakes/seeds), Garam Masala or curry powder, garlic (fresh/salt/granules/paste), ground ginger, mixed herbs, tarragon.

★ Thin with milk, cream, yoghurt or wine.

★ Use mayonaise for the deluxe version.

★ Try Marseilles Mud. Use mayonaise as above half and half with tomato ketchup and add $\frac{1}{4}$ of the amount of French or Dijon mustard. It really looks like mud but tastes dreamy and is an excellent instant mustard sauce for chicken, pork or steak as well as all the items listed under Thousand Mud-Flat Dressing.

YOGHURT WITH GINGER

This little number makes a lovely dip with cheese straws, raw vegetables cut in thin julienne strips or as a pour-over sauce for vegetable salad. The stronger flavours of the malt extract and ginger make it quite different from Cucumber Cooly (*see* p. 74).

WHAT YOU NEED
(per person)

Malt extract $\frac{1}{2}$ tbsp
Yoghurt $\frac{1}{3}$ cup ($\frac{2}{3}$ if used as a dip)
Seasoning
Ginger   Scant $\frac{1}{8}$ tsp (mash root ginger in a garlic press)
Vanilla   Just 1 drop

WHAT YOU DO

Warm the malt extract in a measuring cup standing in hot water or very gently over a burner. Add the vanilla and ginger and mix till well blended. Stir into the yoghurt.

★ *VARIATIONS* ★

★ If using to coat a vegetable salad, add 1 teaspoon of ground Coriander or seeds first.

CONFECTIONERS' CUSTARD

In the ordinary way they'll be darned lucky to get dessert at all, let alone with a sauce to pour over it. But if you're determined to ruin them for ever try this.

WHAT YOU NEED
(for 2)

Milk   1 cup
Honey   2 tbsp
Eggs   2 yolks (use the whites for Yoghurt Snow or
   Souflette)
Cornflour   1 tbsp
Vanilla   1 tsp

WHAT YOU DO

Put the milk on to heat gently. Beat the honey into the egg yolks so they go light and creamy and gradually stir in the cornflour. Pour on the hot (but not boiling) milk and stir to blend. Return the custard to the pan and cook over the lowest heat till thickened, about 4–5 minutes. Allow to cool a little before stirring in the vanilla.

Use over fruit, pastries, trifles, etc. If you're feeling really extravagant add a small carton of cream when the custard is cool. On the other hand you could open a tin, but it ain't the same.

Starters

There can be few cooks afloat who offer a starter as a regular item. But sometimes, at a peaceful anchorage or even back at the marina, you may have guests for dinner or there's something to celebrate – there must be SOMETHING to celebrate – or perhaps you're just feeling indulgent. Try Cabbage Cream – it's wicked on the calories but how often do you serve a starter?

CABBAGE CREAM

WHAT YOU NEED
(per person)

White cabbage $\frac{1}{2}$ cup finely shredded
Cream $\frac{1}{8}$ cup double cream
Seasoning
Pepper $\frac{1}{2}$ tsp, fresh ground or multi-coloured
Salt

WHAT YOU DO

Shred the cabbage very fine using 'Jaws' with the narrow toothed insert, or a very large sharp knife on a board. The finer you can cut the cabbage the better. If using a knife, cut across long shreds to reduce the pieces to no larger than $\frac{1}{4}''$ (6 mm). Put the cabbage into a serving dish and pour over the double cream and the pepper and mix well to coat the cabbage. Taste it and see if it needs a little salt and add as you think fit. Either serve at the table or turn into individual dishes. Garnish with something bright like thin shreds of red pepper or dill seeds.

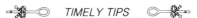 *TIMELY TIPS*

● Don't forget the paper napkins as people tend to gorge themselves on this dish and the cream goes everywhere. Food of the Gods . . . and Heaven doesn't come much simpler than this.

★ *VARIATIONS* ★

★ If you're low on cabbage try adding an unpeeled apple, also shredded fine on 'Jaws' or with a knife.

★ Add fine shreds of sweet red pepper or carrot or both and include a shake of cayenne.

★ Add chopped walnuts to all the above and throw in some dried mixed fruit for a near relative to a Waldorf salad.

★ Vary the seasoning – try dill pepper or citrus pepper, but *plenty* of it.

SAMBOL

This isn't a starter on its own so much as an accompaniment to curry. Its cooling qualities make it a nice foil for any really hot dish, being something like a fresh fruit pickle.

WHAT YOU NEED
(for 4)

Apple 1 unpeeled but chopped very fine or grated
Sweet onion or spring onion 1 tbsp shredded in the smallest pieces
Mixed dried fruit $\frac{1}{4}$ cup
Vinegar/lemon juice $\frac{1}{2}$ tbsp
Sugar $\frac{1}{2}$ tbsp (preferably brown)
Seasoning
Cardamom or mixed spice 1 pinch

WHAT YOU DO

Mix the finely chopped apple and onion and add the dried fruit and seasoning. Sprinkle the vinegar over and stir, which will stop the apple from going brown.

This is another dish where the finer the ingredients are chopped the better the effect. Each person puts a tablespoonful of the Sambol on the side of their plate along with the curry and dips into it as desired.

★ *VARIATIONS* ★

★ If you have no sweet or spring onion you can substitute the smallest amount of ordinary onion shredded like gossamer – to reduce its bite, soak in a little milk and drain before adding.
★ Any fruit is nice as long as it's very thinly sliced into tiny bits. Try apricot, peach or banana and vary the *seasoning* by adding some caraway seeds.

CUCUMBER COOLY

This silky salad is a dream at the end of a hot day as a starter or as a side dish to anything spicy like a curry or chilli.

WHAT YOU NEED
(per person)

Cucumber About $\frac{1}{4}$ of a cucumber
Honey $\frac{1}{2}$ tsp
Yoghurt $\frac{1}{2}$ cup
Seasoning
Rosemary 1 pinch

WHAT YOU DO

Grate the cucumber on 'Jaws' or chop into tiny cubes. Do not skin. Blend the honey into the yoghurt; use clear honey, or warm 'set' honey till it's runny. Add the rosemary and pour over the cucumber. Garnish with something contrasting but mild, like paprika or a sprinkle of rosemary.

CHEESE CRISPS

Amaze your friends and serve these quick and easy nibbles with a glass of wine or beer at the end of a good day and the beginning of a good meal. I stole the recipe from a Dutch sea-wife in Larnaca. If you read this, Hollandaise, please forgive me.

WHAT YOU NEED
(makes 12–15 crisps)

Cheese 1 cup, grated (Cheddar is best)
Butter $\frac{1}{2}$ cup
Flour (plain) $\frac{1}{3}$ cup
Seasoning
Cayenne A liberal pinch
Salt if you're using milder cheese

WHAT YOU DO

Just put the whole lot into a bowl and mix well to form a solid mass. Take a teaspoonful of the mix and drop onto a non-stick baking sheet and squash it flat with a spatula. Do the same with the rest of the mix and cook in a hot oven (425°F/220°C/GM7) for 10–12 minutes. They go bubbly and frilly around the edges and when cooled are crisp and moreish.

★ *VARIATIONS* ★

★ If you really want to show off you can form them round a wooden spoon handle before they harden, like brandy snaps. You can also use them flat as a base for canapés or sandwiched together with soft cheese and a segment of mandarin orange.

MOCK PEANUTS

This is one big cheat, but if you're out of roasted peanuts to nibble with pre-prandial drinks (or just plain mean) try this.

WHAT YOU NEED

Fat or oil Enough to fry
Chick-peas, cooked 1 cup if you're serving other
things, or more if it's all you've got

Seasoning
Chilli seasoning
Salt

WHAT YOU DO

Heat a little oil in a heavy pan or wok over a low heat. Throw in the cooked chick-peas and fry gently until golden brown. Drain on kitchen paper, put into serving bowl and dust with salt and chilli seasoning. Serve at once. If you have any left over you could always add them to a hot dish to jazz it up.

Snacks

If you are a reluctant cook like me, then you probably have a host of 'snack' ideas because it's what our minds tend to turn to when the stomach calls for attention. Making a snack never seems quite so daunting or dedicated as a full meal and I think I must have lived on snacks for years until the demands of a family insisted I enlarge my repertoire. But here is one old stand-by that continues to get me out of trouble. I gave my electric sandwich-maker away and reverted to this method of making toasted sandwiches as it's so simple and the pan is easy to wash, unlike the machine. If you already know this one, skip to the next item.

'TOASTED' SANDWICHES

WHAT YOU NEED
(per person)

Bread   2 slices cut thick or they'll come back for more
Margarine   Enough to spread on each slice
Filling   Whatever you like (I list some ideas below)
Seasoning
You're on your own, but do add *something*

WHAT YOU DO

Butter the slices of bread and place buttered side DOWN in a heavy pan over gentle heat. Put the filling on top of each piece, add seasoning and cover with the second slice, butter side UP. Cover pan and cook for 3–4 minutes until underside is golden brown. (I know it's difficult to tell, but you can sneak a look with the fish slice, then next time you'll be able to guess.) Turn carefully so as not to spill the filling and press the top slice down to squidge the filling into the bread. Cook until the second side is done. Serve.

FILLINGS

● Cheese – most sorts, sliced thin; you can be quite mean if you fill in with seasoning.
● Try a smear of French mustard or tomato ketchup on the top of the first slice before laying on the cheese.
● Any preserved sausage with a thin slice of cheese; this needs no extra seasoning as the garlic sausage is usually highly spiced.
● Thin slices of tomato and wafers of onion. If you can get the sweet white onion be a bit more heavy handed.
● Thinly sliced mushroom and tomato and a micro-sprinkle of mixed herbs.
● A lightly fried egg – it will finish cooking when you turn the sandwich.

SWEET TOASTIES

Exactly the same principle but with a sweet filling; use unsalted butter if you have it. Suggested fillings:

- A dessertspoonful of any jam, marmalade or pie filling.
- A dessertspoonful of stewed fruit sprinkled with mixed spice.
- Sliced banana, sprinkled with cinnamon and brown sugar.
- Thinly sliced dessert apple, sprinkle of cloves and brown sugar.

Everybody's hungry, the larder is bare except for some bread, but not enough cheese to go round. DON'T PANIC, just give them:

JANE'S RAREBIT

. . . or good old Cheese on Toast!

WHAT YOU NEED
(per person)

Bread   1 thick slice
Flour   1 tbsp
Margarine   1 tbsp
Milk $\frac{1}{4}$ cup
Cheese   Anything hard or semi-hard, 1 tbsp grated
Seasoning
Sesame or garlic salt, ground pepper,
Herbes de Provence   1 pinch of each.
Paprika or Crunchy Topping   (*see* page 45)

WHAT YOU DO

Start the bread toasting. Then, employing the foolproof method (*see* p. 66) use the flour, margarine and milk to make a plain sauce. Into this put all the grated cheese and stir till blended. Add the seasoning and taste the result; if it seems bland add more salt and pepper (*see* Variations for additional seasoning). Spread each slice of toast with the cheese sauce and sprinkle liberally with paprika before browning under a hot grill.

TIMELY TIPS

● What we are trying to achieve is some flavour in what is otherwise a rather mean cheese sauce. This is done by the abundant use of seasoning.

● The sauce should be fairly thick so that it doesn't run off the bread too fast. If you do the browning on an enamel or Pyrex plate then sauce that runs off the toast can be scooped back on again.

● The top will brown nicely under a hot grill. If you can't be bothered, or haven't a grill, put more paprika on top.

★ *VARIATIONS* ★

The above is the basic recipe to which you may add whatever you like and as much as you like.

★ For extra seasoning try a dash of Worcestershire sauce or soy sauce, cayenne pepper, chilli seasoning, curry powder or first spread the toast with mustard before putting on the sauce.

★ Try adding any leftover vegetables, chopped very small (chopped mushrooms need no cooking). Just throw them in making sure they are well covered with sauce before grilling.

★ Slice that last moth-eaten tomato (after removing the not-so-nice-bits) in tiny pieces and add it at the last moment. Or slice it in thin rings and top each piece of bread as a garnish, adding Herbes de Provence as additional seasoning.

★ Sliced olives, green or black, are delicious.

★ If you're not grilling, top with Crunchy Topping (*see* chapter on Seasoning) and a good dash of fresh ground pepper.

★ 1 slice of streaky bacon will do 4 people if you chop it small and sprinkle it on top so that all the pieces are visible. The same goes for a little pepperoni.

★ Top it with a poached egg and it's Jane's Buck Rarebit.

EGGY BREAD

'You must know THIS one' I said to someone the other day. But they didn't so here it is – my way. If you know it, skip it.

WHAT YOU NEED
(for 2)

Eggs   1
Bread   2 slices
Butter   2 tbsps
Seasoning
Salt, Pepper

WHAT YOU DO

Beat the egg in a shallow dish. If you want to eke out the egg for three people (or two greedy ones) add a little milk. Dip each piece of bread quickly into the beaten egg and fry immediately in the butter till golden on both sides. When the bread is cooked, season with a little salt and a good turn of the pepper mill.

★ *VARIATIONS* ★

★ Spread a smear of Marmite or Vecon on the bread before dipping in the egg. Sprinkle with cayenne pepper or paprika.

★ Spread a smear of golden syrup or honey on the bread before dipping and frying. Sprinkle with Spiced Sugar (see page 45).

★ Try covering the egged bread in breadcrumbs before frying, which gives it a lovely crunchy texture. This might be going a bit far just for a 'snack', but it's worth the energy.

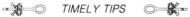 *TIMELY TIPS*

● Cook straight with a light sprinkling of salt but no pepper. Cut into 'fingers' to encourage the seasick sufferers to eat a little something.

SOUFFLETTES

These are really just fluffy omelettes which can be plain or with a variety of fillings.

WHAT YOU NEED
(per person)

Eggs 2
Butter 1 tbsp
Fillings see next page

WHAT YOU DO

Separate the egg whites from the yolks. Beat the whites until fairly stiff; beat the yolks separately and gently combine the two. Heat a heavy pan – it really must be a heavy pan – with a lid and melt the butter over medium heat. Drop in enough of the fluffy mix to nearly fill the bottom of the pan and cover. Cook gently until the underside is set. Carefully fold one half of the soufflette over on to the other and continue cooking with the cover on for another 5 minutes or so. Serve immediately on a warmed plate garnished with Parmesan or chopped parsley if you have them.

FILLINGS

Light fillings are laid on one half of the soufflette just before the other half is folded over.

● Grated cheese and a sprinkle of pepper – the cheese should have melted to a soft goo by the time the soufflette is fully cooked.
● Brown breadcrumbs mixed with finely chopped anchovy fillets and a little ground bayleaf.
● Beansprouts and a sprinkle of Chinese Five Spice.
● Tomatoes and mushrooms, finely chopped, with a little salt, pepper and basil if you like it.

 *TIMELY TIPS*
● Always add salt to egg *after* cooking or it will toughen.

SAVOURIES

The recipes in this section are for main meals and, as I believe everything should do at least two things to earn its place afloat (or ashore), I have given the variations. Nearly all the recipes can be made in several different ways, which means that you can glance through to see which version suits your crew or the contents of the food locker. Who knows, it may spark off ideas for your own improvisation – I don't think I've ever followed a recipe to the letter. Where you might be short on ingredients or not have enough because of an expansive invitation for the entire anchorage to eat aboard by You-Know-Who, I have given ideas for padding out. You can often pad out a dish with brown breadcrumbs or bran, and this is a good way to expand a burger mix or retrieve many a savoury casserole style dish that looks a little too sloppy. Just remember to add more seasoning. You can also use bran to coat burgers, chicken pieces, chops etc. prior to frying to give a crispy coating.

It is worth keeping a supply of cooked beans on hand if you know there are going to be a lot of mouths to feed. Beans (and under this general term are included all the dried beans, peas and pulses) are easily prepared, and after cooking will keep for several days covered in a fridge or at least 2–3 days in a cool place. Rinsing and draining them daily delays them from going sour if unrefrigerated (see Cooking Dried Beans page 120).

Cooked beans can be added to nearly any dish of vegetables or pasta to provide bulk and protein; add the appropriate seasoning and some liquid to make a tasty meal in minutes. Most leading supermarkets do their own range of bean mixes; my local one has a mix with seven different beans making a distictive dish. Using my 'basket' method of pressure cooking, the beans stay colourful and separate, and when cold make an eye-pleasing salad with a few extras.

MIXED BEAN AND VEGETABLE CASSEROLE

This easy dish is a satisfying meal and you can use any vegetables you have to hand so the variations are endless.

WHAT YOU NEED
(for 4)

Onion   1 large or 2 small
Garlic   1 clove or 1 tsp purée/granules
Butter   1 tbsp
Vegetables   2 cups chopped (your choice, mixed)
Flour   2 tbsp
Stock   2 cups of water and 2 stock cubes
Cooked mixed beans   2 cups
Cheese $\frac{1}{2}$ cup grated
Crisps   1 small packet, smashed
Seasoning
Herbes de Provence   1 tsp
Bayleaf, ground   1 tsp
Pepper $\frac{1}{2}$ tsp

WHAT YOU DO

Start the chopped onion and garlic cooking in the butter in a large heavy pan with a close-fitting lid. Chop the rest of the vegetables into proportional sizes; that is, the longer they take to cook the smaller you chop them, i.e. carrots smaller than pota-toes. When the onions are transparent add the flour and mix until it is hot, then add a little stock and cook to thicken. Add the rest of the stock, vegetables and seasoning. Cover and allow to simmer gently until the vegetables are half cooked and then add the bean mix and continue cooking until the vegetables are ready. Serve and top each serving with grated cheese and smashed crisps mixed together.

● This is an excellent dish for the pressure cooker. Start the onion in the base of the cooker, and when you have added the vegetables close the lid and bring to full pressure. Cooking time should be gauged for the toughest vegetable. When cooked release the steam slowly. Remove the lid, add cooked beans, replace the lid and allow to steam for a further few minutes to heat the beans. Serve as above. The length of time cooking at pressure could be as little as 5 minutes if the vegetables are chopped small.

EASY 'SHEPHERD'S PIE'

If you're looking for a quick substantial meal this is it – as long as you already have those cooked beans. This is a good tempered dish that will wait and wait.

WHAT YOU NEED
(for 4)

Butter 1 tbsp
Mixed beans 2 cups, ready cooked
Tomatoes 1 cup creamed tomatoes
Potato 2 cups, mashed (use instant)
Seasoning
Chilli mix 1 tsp
Herbes de Provence 1 tsp
Bayleaf 1 tsp, ground

WHAT YOU DO

Heat the butter and add the seasoning, cooking over a low heat to bring out the flavours. Add the cooked beans and the tomatoes and continue cooking, covered, until well heated. Meanwhile make up the mashed potato as directed. Pour the bean/tomato mix into a casserole and top with the mashed potato, smoothing with a fork to leave tram lines that will brown nicely under the grill.

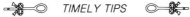

● If the whole thing is good and hot it can be served immediately. If you want to set it up ahead of time (yes, it does happen once in a while) pop it in a moderate oven (350°F/180°C/GM4) about 30 minutes or so before you want to serve it.

★ *VARIATIONS* ★

★ Instead of creamed tomatoes try any of the wide variety of cooking sauces in packets and cartons.

★ Instead of mixed beans, try mixed vegetables, chopped small and add chopped boiled egg for protein.

JANE'S AMAZING LENTIL LOAF

This recipe is one of my favourites. It's a doddle to make and is very adaptable. It keeps very well – in fact it tastes better the next day. It cuts well cold and I freeze it ready sliced separated with greaseproof paper. I've given variations and I'm sure you can invent more for yourself. It's a quick recipe because lentils, unlike beans, don't need soaking overnight nor rapid boiling.

WHAT YOU NEED
(for 4–6)

Red lentils $\frac{2}{3}$ cup
Carrot   1 large, coarse grated
Garlic   1 clove, finely chopped or crushed
Onion   1 finely chopped
Hard cheese $\frac{1}{2}$ cup grated
Egg   1 large
Seasoning
Bayleaf   1 pinch of ground, not leaf
Chilli seasoning   1 tsp commercial mixes like
Season-All
Pepper

WHAT YOU DO

Boil the lentils till half done (10 minutes or less) then add the grated carrots, garlic and onion. Stop cooking just before the lentils are fully cooked – that is, while they still have an 'eye' in the middle. Drain. Stir in the grated cheese, ground bay leaf and season heavily (remember the chapter on Seasoning?) – what ever you like but lots of pepper. My standby is Season-All by Schwartz. Add the egg and beat it all. Slop it into a buttered or non-stick loaf tin and bake 40–45 minutes (400°F/200°C/GM6).

   *TIMELY TIPS*

● Don't overcook! It should look a little soggy in the middle; don't bother with the toothpick test, either. Give it 10 minutes to rest or it'll fall apart when you slice it. The trick is not to allow the lentils to break up, or they become mushy.

● If this does happen, you can always purée the whole lot, add water and a stock cube and call it Bounty Broth.

● DO TASTE IT before baking to see if it needs any salt, and add as necessary; only you can judge that. Try adding celery salt.

● Be warned – because of the garlic, cover the loaf tightly and seal in a container before storing in your cool place or the fridge.

★ *VARIATIONS* ★

★ Microwave 7 minutes on full. To cook in the pressure cooker, cover with well secured foil or greaseproof paper and stand on a trivet with 1 pint (600 ml) of water and cook for 14–15 minutes at full pressure.

★ If you're short on ingredients or have unexpected diners just as you're making it, throw in a cup of brown breadcrumbs or bran or more carrot. If you're out of carrot, try grated parsnip – not so colourful but tasty. Add more seasoning to compensate for the extra bulk.

★ This mix, with the breadcrumbs, is stiffer and will make nice Burgers to fry, with or without a coating of crumbs or brown flour.

★ Try Lentil Wellington, rolled in pastry. Slash the top to let the steam escape and brush with milk. Bake on a tray.

★ Or mixed with curry powder wrapped in flaky pastry as Curry Puffs.

★ Fill Vol-au-Vents (ready-made or use instant puff pastry) if you're trying to impress; decorate with sliced olive. If you have the pastry add a good dash of chilli sauce or chilli seasoning mix and make Sausage Rolls with it.

★ Add a generous dollop of tomato paste to the mix, pack it well down in a pastry case, dot the top with sliced olives and thin strips of anchovy, bake for 20 minutes and call it Pan Pizza.

★ Or make Cheat'n Pizza, with a thick slice of brown toast spread generously with the hot cooked tomato mix, topped with cheese and a sprinkling of paprika and grilled until the cheese bubbles.

★ Individual thin slices can be taken straight from the freezer and fried until hot and crispy, topped with cheese, egg or bacon and slid between two pieces of bread for a satisfying quick snack.

★ Add a good dash of Worcestershire sauce and pack into a round pie dish, top with mashed potato (instant or otherwise), sprinkle with paprika and bake. If the loaf mix and the potato are both hot it is only necessary to brown the potato topping under the grill.

GILLIE'S EGGY LENTIL BURGERS

WHAT YOU NEED
(for 2 large or 3 medium burgers)

Egg   1 hard boiled and chopped
Lentils $\frac{1}{2}$ cup
Onion $\frac{1}{2}$ cup, chopped small
Flour   Enough, brown, for coating
Seasoning
Parsley   2 tbsp, fresh or dried
Worcestershire sauce   1 dash
Salt and pepper $\frac{1}{4}$ tsp of each

WHAT YOU DO

Put the egg on to hard boil, if not already cooked. Simmer lentils in 1 cup of water, topping it up so that the lentils absorb all the water and cook dry. Meanwhile, fry the onions until soft. Shell and chop the egg, mix with other ingredients – except the flour – and shape into burgers. Coat with flour and fry on both sides until crisp and brown.

NUT BURGERS

WHAT YOU NEED
In equal parts (1 cup of mix makes 2 meal-sized burgers)

Peanuts $\frac{1}{2}$ cup crushed
Stuffing mix $\frac{1}{2}$ cup country herb or stuffing mix.
Brown breadcrumbs or **Flour**
Seasoning
Garlic salt

WHAT YOU DO

Mix the crushed peanuts and stuffing mix and add a good shake of garlic salt. Mix with sufficient hot water to give a workable but soft dough. Form into burgers about $\frac{1}{2}''$ (12 mm) thick, roll in brown breadcrumbs or brown flour and fry gently till crispy on both sides.

★ *VARIATIONS* ★

★ If you're feeling extravagant you could try walnuts, hazelnuts, Brazils, or a mix, but they'll need plenty of seasoning to make up for the salt of the peanuts. On the other hand, if you're not feeling extravagant or there are extra crew for supper, this is another recipe that will stand padding with brown breadcrumbs. But please don't forget to increase the seasoning to cope with the extra bulk. You could try Chinese Five Spice/chilli/cayenne pepper.

★ Chestnuts, cooked and mashed, make a lovely burger; you could sanction a tin of purée for a special occasion as cooking chestnuts is not the greatest fun afloat. Or take some from that batch you cooked and froze so thoughtfully last Christmas.

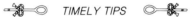 *TIMELY TIPS*

● Put ordinary salted peanuts in a tough plastic bag and use the rolling pin to break them up. You can do them in a blender at home and store them in an air-tight container for later use. Remember, nuts have a high fat content so they need to be kept cool and not stored for too long. Nuts go rancid quickly which is bad for you.

BEANBURGERS

Hot and spicy, these beanburgers make a meal in themselves, slid in between a soft brown roll or served with potatoes and vegetables. Cabbage Cream (see page 72) is a nice accompaniment either way.

WHAT YOU NEED
(for 2 burgers)

Onion 1 small
Carrot 1 small, shredded
Mixed beans 1 cup, ready cooked
Milk $\frac{1}{4}$ cup to mix
Flour $\frac{1}{4}$ cup to coat
Oil 1 tbsp
Seasoning
Chilli seasoning mix 1 tsp
Pepper $\frac{1}{2}$ tsp fresh ground or pepper mix (dill)
Salt

WHAT YOU DO

Chop half the onion finely, slice the rest into rings. Start the small pieces cooking with the shredded carrot very slowly while you mash the beans roughly with the seasoning. Add the pepper, part cooked onion and carrot to the beans and bind with a little milk to form a firm paste. Form into burgers and press in flour all over before frying gently till brown on both sides. Fry the onion rings and use them to garnish the burgers.

TIMELY TIPS

● Mash the beans only enough to break them up to make them easier to bind into a burger.

● If the cooked bean mix is a little dry add a small amount of oil and boiling water instead of milk to help bind it.

● There's no real need to coat burgers with flour prior to frying, but brown flour makes them nice and crisp on the outside. For the De Luxe Burger coat with Crunchy Topping then fry.

VEGETABLE CHEESE CRUMBLE

Use the pastry mix for Cheesey Scones (*see* chapter on Breads) but omit the water to make a tasty cheesey crumble topping for leftover vegetables.

WHAT YOU NEED
(per person)

Vegetables $\frac{2}{3}$ cup, ready cooked
Stock $\frac{1}{4}$ cup water with one vegetable cube
Crumble $\frac{1}{3}$ cup, using recipe on page 154
Seasoning
Celery salt $\frac{1}{4}$ tsp
Herbes de Provence 1 pinch

WHAT YOU DO

Simply put chopped cooked vegetables and stock into the casserole, stir in the seasoning and top with the crumble mix. Bake in a hot oven (425°F/220°C/GM7) for 35–40 minutes.

★ *VARIATIONS* ★

★ If using fresh vegetables chop small with 'Jaws' and throw into a pan of boiling water while you prepare the crumble. Drain the vegetables and put them into a casserole dish. Season the cooking water and thicken it with a little arrowroot before pouring over the vegetables. Top with the cheesy crumble and bake.

★ If you're feeling really indulgent you can make a cheese sauce to coat the vegetables before topping with the crumble.

★ For different seasoning try chilli mix/Season-All/garlic salt and ground pepper/Herbes de Provence or a little ground bayleaf.

TIMELY TIPS

● If you are a little short on quantity you can pad out with breadcrumbs, lentils, pasta, rice, instant potato (all these ready-cooked/leftovers), or chopped raw mushrooms which will cook in the juice of the casserole.

● Cracked wheat will bulk out the casserole but you will need to increase the liquid as the wheat soaks up quite a bit.

CARROT SURPRISE

This is really a soufflé but I didn't dare say so right out in case you got scared. This really works, no problem, and the ginger lifts it out of the norm. Use young spring carrots for a tasty meal served with Melba Toast or crispbread and a simple salad.

WHAT YOU NEED
(for 4–6)

Carrots 2 cups, grated
Butter 3 tbsp
Flour $\frac{1}{4}$ cup
Ginger 1 grape-sized piece of stem ginger chopped
           very small or $\frac{1}{2}$ tsp of powdered ginger
Eggs 3 large
Cheese 1 tbsp, grated

WHAT YOU DO

Throw the grated carrots into boiling water and cook till soft enough to push through a coarse sieve, saving the carrot water. Make a sauce with the butter, flour and enought carrot water to thicken using my foolproof method (see page 66) and mix in the carrot purée and ginger. Now taste it. Add a little salt if you think it's too bland. Set it aside to cool.

Separate the egg whites and whisk until 'peaky', then beat the yolks in a mug. (This way round you don't have to wash the whisk.) Add the beaten egg to the carrots and gently fold in the whites using a metal spoon so as to retain as much air as possible. Turn the whole lot into a non-stick straight sided dish, sprinkle with cheese and bake in a hot oven (400°F/200°C/GM6) for 30 minutes or so.

This soufflé is cooked when it is set and the joy is that it doesn't collapse on you. The tiny pieces of finely grated root ginger, if used, make this dish rather special.

SHRIMP CREOLE

WHAT YOU NEED
(per person)

Oil 1 tbsp
Shrimp $\frac{1}{4}$ cup at least, or more if you've got it
Onion $\frac{1}{4}$ sliced chunky
Green pepper $\frac{1}{8}$ cup, chopped small
Mushrooms $\frac{1}{4}$ cup, chopped small
Tomatoes 1 chopped small
Shrimp sauce 1 tsp
Oyster sauce 1 tsp
Bean sprouts 1 cup

WHAT YOU DO

Heat the oil in a wok or thick fry-pan. Stir fry all the ingredients in the order given, but leaving the shrimp till last. Add a little water to make more sauce if desired. Serve with fluffy rice spiked with a little lemon juice.

 *TIMELY TIPS*

● This recipe is best with fresh shrimp which you've bought from that nice Old Salt on the wharf, but tinned will do.
● If you don't have shrimp or oyster sauce you can use soy, but it's worth putting oyster sauce on the shopping list – you'll use it in other dishes. It's obtainable at most food stores or delicatessens.

FAST LENTIL CURRY

This is a meal in minutes and, served with brown bread if you haven't got time or energy to do rice, makes a whole protein meal. Delicious with mango chutney.

WHAT YOU NEED
(per person)

Red lentils $\frac{1}{3}$ cup
Onion 1 small or 1 large between 2 people
Curry $\frac{1}{2}$ tsp or to taste (*see* chapter on Seasoning)

WHAT YOU DO

Pour boiling water over the lentils and allow to soak for 10 minutes while you peel and slice the onion and start to fry it very, very gently. Rinse the lentils and cook them in twice their volume of water till tender. Do not overcook or they go mushy. Back to the onions – stir in the curry in whatever form you choose and blend it well with the oil and onion until the aroma develops. Drain the cooked lentils and fluff up to allow steam to escape. Turn them into the onion pan and fold the mixes together. Serve with a little grated apple on the side.

PEPPER POT MUSHROOMS

Here's another hot spicy dish and you can cheat and use a small can of red kidney beans and their juice.

WHAT YOU NEED
(per person)

Oil 1 tbsp (preferably olive)
Garlic As much as you like, crushed
Onion 1 small onion, chopped medium
Red kidney beans $\frac{1}{3}$ cup cooked or tinned
Tomato paste $\frac{1}{2}$ tbsp (less if using tinned beans)
Mushrooms $\frac{1}{2}$ cup, chopped into medium pieces
Seasoning
Cayenne pepper $\frac{1}{8}$ tsp
Citrus pepper $\frac{1}{8}$ tsp
or
Freshly ground black pepper

WHAT YOU DO

Gently heat the oil in a heavy pan and sweat the garlic and onion. Add the kidney beans and tomato paste mixed with $\frac{1}{4}$ cup of water per person and the seasoning. If using canned beans in a sauce then reduce the water accordingly. Allow the mixture to simmer gently and then add the mushrooms and continue to simmer, adding more water if the mixture appears too dry.

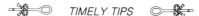 *TIMELY TIPS*

● This dish should be as hot as hell so remember to taste it before serving ɔ make sure you've put enough seasoning in.
● Do not over ɔok the mushrooms; they hardly need more than heating throuɡ n and should not be soft or mushy.

DEE'S HERBY LENTIL CASSEROLE

This casserole, like other recipes needing a longer cooking time, is best made at a quiet anchorage or ashore. But it is a warming dish to round off a spring or autumn sailing day. Brown rolls are a good accompaniment as they can be used to wipe out the bowls and thereby assist with the washing-up.

WHAT YOU NEED
(for 4)

Red lentils $\frac{3}{4}$ cup, uncooked
Onion   1 large, chopped
Brown rice $\frac{1}{2}$ cup, uncooked
White wine $\frac{1}{4}$ cup
Water $2\frac{2}{3}$ cups
Mozzarella cheese   3 tbsp grated
Seasoning
Herbes de Provence   1 tsp
Garlic powder $\frac{1}{4}$ tsp or 1 clove, crushed

WHAT YOU DO

Combine all the ingredients (except the cheese) in an ungreased casserole dish and bake uncovered in a moderate oven (350°F/180°C/GM4) for about $1\frac{1}{2}$ hours. The dish should look moist but not runny. Spread the cheese over the top and return to the oven for another 5 minutes.

★ *VARIATIONS* ★

★ Vegetables such as tomatoes and green peppers can be added for more colour and variety.
★ If you have cooked rice left over, use it and reduce the cooking time to 50 minutes.
★ For pressure cooking, cover the dish with foil/greaseproof paper and secure. Stand the dish on a trivet with 1 pint (600 ml) of water and cook for 30 minutes at full pressure.

PASTA PRIMAVERA

Springtime Pasta! Let your imagination be your guide to adding or substituting other quick cooking vegetables.

WHAT YOU NEED
(for 4)

Spaghetti $\frac{3}{4}$×1 lb (500 g) packet
Oil 1 tbsp
Garlic 2 cloves, crushed or purée/granules
Onion 1 large, cut into thin wedges
Mushrooms $1\frac{1}{2}$ cups
Broccoli 2 cups in small florets
Courgettes 2 cups sliced
Carrots 1 cup, sliced by 'Jaws' or chopped thin
White wine $\frac{1}{2}$ cup
Cheese $\frac{1}{2}$ cup grated
Parsley $\frac{1}{2}$ cup chopped
Seasoning
Basil 2 tsp
Pepper $\frac{1}{8}$ tsp ground
Salt 1 tsp or less

WHAT YOU DO

Start the spaghetti cooking in boiling water. Meanwhile, heat the oil in a wok or heavy pan over medium heat. Add the garlic then onion and mushroom, stirring frequently, and cook for 1–2 minutes. Add the broccoli, courgettes and carrots, stirring the while, then add the wine and cook for a further 2–3 minutes or until the vegetables are tender-crisp. Drain the cooked spaghetti and toss it into the vegetable mixture. Serve immediately, topped with cheese and parsley.

This makes a very generous serving for 4, and with a little salad and the rest of that white wine should make the world a reasonable place for a while.

VEGETABLES A LA MAROC

If you have some fresh beans and want a change from the usual 'boiled', try this filling Moroccan dish. It's easy to make and can be left to look after itself while you get on with the serious business of drinking.

WHAT YOU NEED
(party size for 6)

Onion   1 large, chopped
Water   2 tbsp
Oil   1 tbsp
Potatoes   2 cups, chopped in large cubes
Carrots   2 cups, chopped in $\frac{1}{2}$″ (12 mm) pieces
Tomatoes   2 cups, chopped
Tomato juice   1 × 1 litre ($1\frac{3}{4}$ pts)
Fresh green beans   2 cups, sliced 2″ (5 cm) pieces
Seasoning
Cumin $\frac{3}{4}$ tsp
Pepper $\frac{1}{4}$ tsp ground black or cayenne (cayenne is
          hotter)

WHAT YOU DO

Simmer the onion in the oil and water until transparent. Add potatoes, carrots, tomato juice and one cup of water and simmer for 15 minutes, stirring occasionally. Add tomatoes and cumin; cover and simmer for about an hour. Check to see if more liquid is required; if so add extra water. Add the green beans and cook till done, (about 15 minutes). TASTE IT. Add a little more cumin or pepper if you think the crew can take it.

MACARONI BAKE

This is a low calorie dish and is nice as a complete meal with salad and brown bread or as an accompaniment to chicken or sausages.

WHAT YOU NEED
(for 4)

Macaroni 2 cups, dried
Onion 1 large chopped
Margarine 2 tbsp
Flour $\frac{1}{4}$ cup brown or white, SR or plain
Milk 2 cups, skimmed (full cream milk adds calories)
Cottage cheese 2 cups or 1 large carton
Breadcrumbs $\frac{1}{3}$ cup
Paprika Enough to sprinkle over the top
Seasoning
Parsley 2 tsp dried flakes
Dill weed 2 tsp
Garlic powder $\frac{1}{8}$ tsp
Pepper $\frac{1}{2}$ tsp
Salt $\frac{1}{2}$ tsp or less

WHAT YOU DO

Start the macaroni cooking. Meanwhile, in a large pan, cook the onion gently in the margarine and stir in the flour, stirring all the time for about 1 minute. Gradually add the milk, stir and cook till thickened. Add the seasoning and the cottage cheese and mix well. Tip the cooked, drained macaroni into the sauce and turn it over gently to mix it well. Turn into a shallow casserole, top with the breadcrumbs and sprinkle with paprika before baking in a medium oven (375°C/190°C/GM5) for 30 minutes.

★ *VARIATIONS* ★

★ If all the ingredients are piping hot, turn into individual flameproof dishes, top with the breadcrumbs and toast under a medium grill till browned.
★ If you can't be bothered with breadcrumbs just smash a packet of crisps into small crumbs and sprinkle those on top; grill till browned.

BASIC BOLOGNESE

This bolognese sauce uses wholewheat, with its chewy texture, to replace the standard minced beef – it's a lot cheaper too. With the complimentary protein in the cheese topping it is a complete meal with pasta and a side salad and fresh fruit for dessert. Remember $\frac{3}{4}$ cup of pasta per person (1 cup with larger pasta shapes like quills). Buon appetito!

WHAT YOU NEED
(per person)

Wholewheat $\frac{1}{3}$ cup, cooked, or a scant $\frac{1}{4}$ cup uncooked
Garlic $\frac{1}{2}$ clove, crushed or chopped
Olive oil   for frying
Onion $\frac{1}{2}$ chopped small
Tomato $\frac{1}{2}$ cup of tomatoes in a carton, or 2 whole
fresh, chopped + $\frac{1}{4}$ cup water, or 1 tbsp
tomato purée (tube) + $\frac{1}{3}$ cup water
Mushrooms $\frac{1}{4}$ cup, chopped small or 1 tbsp dried
Cheese   grated for topping
Seasoning
Oregano   What else? 1 good pinch per person ($\frac{1}{8}$ tsp)
Pepper

WHAT YOU DO

Cook the wholewheat grains by simmering in water until tender – about 30 minutes – or use the pressure cooker for 6–7 minutes. Cook the crushed garlic in a heavy pan with a little olive oil and add the onions; cover and let them sweat. Add the tomato, mushrooms and oregano. Stir and cover, allowing the mixture to brew gently to bring out the herb flavour. Add the cooked, drained wholewheat, mix well and heat through. Serve over spaghetti or any other pasta, and cover generously with grated cheese – Parmesan if you have it – and a liberal grind of fresh pepper.

TIMELY TIPS

● With the tomato purée in a tube you will need to add at least $\frac{1}{3}$ cup of water for each person. Add half, stir and see how it looks; add more if the mix is too stiff. Bolognese sauce should be fairly sloppy in order to coat the pasta thoroughly and flick over the assembled company when twirled on a fork. With the fresh tomato you may want to thicken with a little arrowroot to get the right flicking consistency.

LASAGNA

Use the previous recipe, with some grated cheese, to make a lasagna. The instant lasagna sheets mentioned in the section on Packets, sachets, etc. in the Victualling chapter guarantee success.

WHAT YOU NEED
(for 4)

Basic Bolognese   2 cups (see previous recipe)
Instant wholewheat lasagna   6 sheets
Cheese   2 cups, grated
Seasoning
Pepper   1 tsp

WHAT YOU DO

Make up the Basic Bolognese and add 2 cups of water to make a fairly sloppy sauce as this non-cook lasagna soaks up quite a bit of liquid. Starting with the sauce, layer the instant wholewheat sheets, the Bolognese and the cheese in a casserole dish, making sure the top layer of lasagna is well wetted. Top with grated cheese and bake for 30 minutes in a moderately hot oven (375°F/190°C/GM5), or stand the dish, covered with well secured greaseproof paper, on a trivet in a pressure cooker and give it 12 minutes at full pressure. Brown under the grill or sprinkle with paprika.

   TIMELY TIPS

● The sheets are square so if your dish is round you'll have to trim the sheets to size, but drop the bits in the middle of the sauce so they can soak up the liquid.

SHEPHERD'S PIE

Here's a good way to use up leftover vegetables. Of course they are not 'left over'; you very efficiently cooked enough at the last meal to provide for this one. This is another of those dishes that will wait once prepared, if necessary.

WHAT YOU NEED
(for 4–6)

Basic Bolognese   2 cups (see recipe on page 96)
Vegetables   2 cups, anything left over
Instant potato $\frac{1}{3}$ cup made with milk or water

WHAT YOU DO

Make the Basic Bolognese and throw in any vegetables, includ-ing potatoes as long as they're all chopped small, and allow to simmer gently to heat the vegetables through. Make up the instant mash as per instructions, using milk and butter for a richer taste if you like.

You can either put the Bolognese vegetables into a casserole and fork the potato over the top and bake for a further 20 minutes in a hot oven (425°F/220°C/GM7), or set it up in individual ramekins and put them under the grill to brown.

EASY PAN PIZZA

This is a pizza you cook in a heavy pan with a lid. It uses pastry instead of yeast dough but is tasty and quicker than the real thing.

WHAT YOU NEED
(for 4)

Basic pastry   see page 145 (or use ready-made)
Oil   2 tbsp
Tomatoes   2 sliced or 1 cup carton tomatoes, drained
Cheese   1 cup, grated
Seasoning
Oregano   1 tsp
Pepper   1 tsp
Garlic $\frac{1}{2}$ tsp granules/salt
Salt $\frac{1}{2}$ tsp

WHAT YOU DO

Make up the pastry and roll or press it out to the size of your heaviest pan. Heat the oil in the pan over a medium heat and lay the pastry in the bottom of the pan. Turn down the heat, cover the pan with a tight lid and cook slowly until the pastry is brown on the underside – about 5 to 7 minutes. Carefully turn the pastry over and arrange the tomato slices on the top (cooked side) of the pizza (or pour over the carton tomatoes if using these). Sprinkle with the oregano, pepper and garlic, adding salt if you are not using garlic salt. Scatter the grated cheese over the top, put the lid back on and continue cooking until the underside of the pastry is cooked and the cheese is melted. Put the whole thing under the grill to brown the cheese if you like. Slice and serve.

≈⊰○ *TIMELY TIPS* ○⊱≈

● This pastry usually holds together quite well. If you haven't made an enormous pizza you should be able to slide it out of the pan on to a plate in one piece, where you will find it easier to slice with kitchen scissors.

● If you're nervous about turning the pastry, slide it out onto a plate, top it with another plate, invert the whole assembly, and slide the pastry back into the pan. The plates are supposed to be oiled but I never found this to be necessary. The plates are clean enough to serve on.

★ *VARIATIONS* ★

★ You can add virtually anything that comes to hand. Mushrooms are the most obvious addition – just chop them small and mix them in with the tomato.

★ Anchovies and olives, black or green, as well as red and green peppers are all good garnish.

★ When adding onion it needs to be cooked first.

★ Try bacon, ham or pepperoni chopped small and sprinkled between the tomato and cheese.

★ Pilchard or sardines (tinned) mashed with the tomatoes and spread under the cheese. A little goes a long way; you might save just enough from the lunchtime sandwiches.

TARTY MARTO

This is a little naughty with the double cream and egg yolks, but it is a rattling good pie and you can always diet tomorrow – or whenever. The French mustard gives a special zing. Serve it with a cooling Cucumber Salad.

WHAT YOU NEED
(for 4)

Tomatoes chopped $\frac{1}{2}$ cup drained
French mustard 2 tbsp, or more if you dare
Pastry shell 1 × 8″ (20 cm) circular
Hard cheese 1 cup when grated (Gruyère or Emmental is best but Cheddar is nearly as nice)
Double cream $\frac{1}{2}$ cup – fresh/tinned/carton
Eggs 2
Seasoning
Herbes de Provence $\frac{1}{2}$ tsp
Ground pepper A good dusting all over the cheese

WHAT YOU DO

Mix the herbs with the chopped tomatoes. Spread the French mustard on the pastry and sprinkle the cheese over – not forgetting the pepper – and pat down before covering with the tomato and herb mix. Combine the double cream with the beaten eggs and pour over to cover all the other ingredients. Bake in a moderate oven (325°F/160°C/GM3) for 45 minutes or until the top is set.

★ *VARIATIONS* ★

★ If the dairy can't oblige with the cream, yoghurt is nearly as good.

VEGETABLE CACHA

I'm not sure that's spelled correctly as I've never seen it written down and no one else has ever heard of the term, which I was led to understand meant, roughly, a collection of things added to rice – sort of risotto, I suppose.

WHAT YOU NEED
(per person)

Oil   1 tsp
Rice $\frac{1}{3}$ cup
Garlic $\frac{1}{4}$ clove or $\frac{1}{4}$ tsp purée
Stock $\frac{1}{2}$ cup water with vegetable cube
Vegetables $\frac{1}{2}$ cup finely chopped
Seasoning
Salt   1 pinch
Oregano   1 good pinch
Pepper mix   1 jolly good pinch

WHAT YOU DO

Heat the oil gently and throw in the rice, garlic and oregano, turning it all with a spatula until the rice is coated. Let the rice heat for a minute or two before adding the stock. Close the lid, lower the heat and simmer till the rice is nearly cooked – about 15 minutes. During this time, chop the vegetables into small pieces. (This won't take all the time so pour yourself a small one and consider your many talents.) When the rice is nearly cooked toss in the vegetables and stir, slam the lid back on and finish your contemplation.

Check to see if the rice is cooked or needs more liquid; if it does add water/beer/wine. Stir in the pepper and TASTE. Ask yourself if it needs a little salt. Ask someone else if it needs a little salt. Consider the evidence and add salt if you think it's necessary.

★ VARIATIONS ★

★ This is a dish that need never turn out the same twice. You can use fresh or leftover vegetables in practically any combination. Ready cooked vegetables only need heating through.

★ Add a small tin of mussels or prawns and call it Paella, or flaked cooked fish and it's Kedgeree.

MIXED BEANS WITH CELERY

WHAT YOU NEED
(per person)

Celery $\frac{1}{4}$ stalk
Cooked mixed beans 1 cup
Walnut oil Enough to coat beans and make them
glisten
Seasoning
Garam Masala $\frac{1}{2}$ tsp

WHAT YOU DO

Chop the celery as fine as possible. Mix with the beans and the Garam Masala, and drizzle on enough walnut oil to put a shine on the beans when mixed in. Garnish with the leaf tips of the celery.

 *TIMELY TIPS*

● It really is worth using the walnut oil as it seems to bring out the best in the Garam Masala, or try hazelnut oil; 'first pressing' olive oil gives a lovely Mediterranean taste; throw in some chopped black olives for good measure.

● If you want the best effect then gently warm the oil in a measuring cup sitting in a mug of boiling water and blend the Garam Masala into it before coating the beans. If you start this off first, the oil will be just right by the time you've sorted the other things.

● Do remember that teaspoon measures are *flat* and $\frac{1}{2}$ teaspoon is a very small quantity. Too much Garam Massala could ruin a good friendship.

MACARONI CHEESE WITH VEGETABLES

Macaroni cheese can be pretty dull in the ordinary way. Here, with the vegetables and wholewheat, you have a complete meal all in one dollop.

WHAT YOU NEED
(per person)

Macaroni $\frac{1}{2}$ cup, uncooked
Butter 1 tbsp
Flour 1 tbsp
Milk $\frac{1}{2}$ cup
Cheese $\frac{1}{3}$ cup, grated Cheddar (can be less if you add more seasoning)
Oil 1 tbsp
Onions $\frac{1}{4}$ cup, rough chopped
Garlic as much as you like, clove/granules/purée
Mushrooms $\frac{1}{4}$ cup, chopped
Tomatoes $\frac{1}{4}$ cup, chopped
Wholewheat $\frac{1}{8}$ cup, cooked
Seasoning
Bayleaf 1 pinch, ground
Mixed herbs 1 pinch
Pepper $\frac{1}{8}$ tsp

WHAT YOU DO

Set the pasta to cook either by the Set Aside method (see page 26) or by simmering gently in salted water. Either way, watch it doesn't overcook – it must be 'al dente'. Meanwhile, use the butter, flour and milk to make a foolproof sauce (see p. 66) and add the cheese to melt. In another pan warm the oil and seasoning then add the onion, garlic, mushrooms and tomatoes and turn gently until the oil is absorbed. Close the lid and simmer until all are just tender – do not overcook to a mush. Add the cooked wholewheat and stir till heated. Combine this mix with the sauce and the cooked, strained pasta and turn till thoroughly coated. Serve with a salad or brown bread or both.

 *TIMELY TIPS*

● Top with crushed crisps or grated cheese or both. Top with Crunchy Topping. Top with chopped parsley.
● It is important not to overcook the pasta and the tomato/mushroom mix or it becomes a sloppy mess.

★ *VARIATIONS* ★

★ Add any other vegetables you have to hand – carrot is nice.
★ You can use any shaped pasta though shells are best.

PASTA AND MUSHROOMS

This recipe works best with fresh mushrooms and the brown skinned ones are perfect. Pick out 2 per person, about $1\frac{1}{2}''$ (4 cm) across. Or use a can of whole button mushrooms, allowing $\frac{1}{2}$ a small can per person. You can make it quickly using a carton or packet of cheese pouring sauce.

WHAT YOU NEED
(per person)

Pasta shells $\frac{3}{4}$ cup or 1 cup if using quills
Butter 1 tbsp plus a little more to cook mushrooms
Milk $\frac{1}{3}$ cup (approx).
Flour 1 tbsp
Cheese $\frac{1}{8}$ cup (a little more if using Edam)
Garlic 1 tsp purée/granules
Mushrooms 2, quartered, or $\frac{1}{2}$ a small can
Seasoning
Dill weed $\frac{1}{2}$ tsp per person
Season-All $\frac{1}{4}$ tsp per person
Citrus pepper To garnish

WHAT YOU DO

Set the pasta to cook. (If you want to use a ready-made cheese sauce go straight to ★.) Meanwhile, make a sauce with the butter, flour and milk using the foolproof method (see page 66) and add the cheese to melt. ★Add the cheese sauce to the cooked drained pasta and cover to keep hot. Melt the rest of the butter and add the dill, Season-All and garlic and allow to warm gently. Add the quartered mushrooms and turn so they take up the butter mixture. Close the lid and gently simmer the mushrooms for 3–4 minutes, turning them periodically. Fold the mushrooms into the pasta and cheese mix until well blended. Serve well showered with the citrus pepper, accompanied by crisp French bread and a light white wine.

 *TIMELY TIPS*

● The sauce for this recipe is as thin as single cream (which you can add to enrichen it) and the flavour is delicate. The joy is in the large chunks of mushroom – which, though cooked, are still firm – wrapped in their dill-flavoured blanket.

VEGETABLES

As a non-cook, I used to think the least of my problems was vegetables. You boil 'em and dish 'em, don't you?

W-e-l-l, yes, and then again, no. It's HOW you boil them and HOW you serve them that makes the difference between that awful green evil smelling mush you were given at school and an Ambrosian feast.

Man took to cooking vegetables because he found they were more digestible and tasted better and it gave him more things he could eat. He also found that the smaller he cut the pieces the quicker they cooked which saved fuel, which is the reason the Chinese developed stir-frying. Also, you only need a fork if everything on your plate is bite size or less, which saves washing-up. All this makes sense on a boat.

Most vegetables benefit from being cooked quickly in the minimum of fluid to make them edible and not allowed to stew after cooking. Better still is steaming which retains colour and goodness. Casseroling is a different method of cooking; here, we are talking about vegetables to be cooked and eaten separately.

Presenting vegetables attractively is rather like being an artist but not so difficult. Even dragging a fork across the top of mashed potato makes it look better, and if you now shake on some paprika it falls into the little troughs and somehow gives the impression that you made the effort.

Finally, before we get down to business, most vegetables improve from the addition of seasoning. This is particularly true afloat where the cook may find herself limited in the choice of vegetables she can offer. No matter; with the addition of some well chosen herbs and spices even the humble potato can assume a variety of different guises.

Generally, I have not given amounts as this section is more about ideas; you are the best judge of how much your crew will eat.

And so to work – but DON'T forget the seasoning.

HARD WHITE CABBAGE WITH GINGER

Slice thinly and steam until cooked but still crunchy having put $\frac{1}{4}$ teaspoon of ground ginger in the cooking water. After draining the cabbage, add a nob of butter and thicken the cooking water with a little cornflour or arrowroot. Pour over the cabbage just before serving. This works well over cauliflower too, if you don't want to bother with a cheese sauce.

★ *VARIATIONS* ★

★ Instead of ginger try a teaspoon of curry powder and thicken the sauce as above.

★ Grate a carrot finely and cook it with the cabbage. The carrot will be crisp and the ginger seasoning goes very well. Add plenty of fresh ground pepper on top.

★ Grate an apple and throw in just a little dried mixed fruit and 1 drop of vanilla in the cooking water to enhance the butter sauce. Substitute a ground clove for the ginger.

★ Shred carrot and apple as well as cabbage and make coleslaw with Thousand Mud-Flat Dressing.

Things to do with potatoes

Always cook more potatoes than you need for the main meal. The rest will come in handy for part of something tomorrow. Remember: there's no such thing as 'left overs'. The correct term is 'precooked'. Likewise, food is never 'burnt', merely 'well done'.

BUBBLE AND SQUEAK

Don't neglect this old-time favourite. It's a wonderful base to which you can add any number of things to make it a complete meal. There are one or two points that will lift it out of the bitter watery mess you might remember as a child.

WHAT YOU NEED
(per person)

Butter   1 tbsp per serving
Potatoes   pre-cooked, ⅔ cup
Greens   Cabbage – or any chopped cooked green
vegetable
Seasoning
Garlic   1 clove, crushed – at least, or purée/granules
Pepper   plenty of fresh ground
Salt   Enough to give the potatoes a bite
Bayleaf   Ground, 1 pinch per serving

WHAT YOU DO

While the butter is gently drawing the best out of the garlic in a heavy pan, roughly chop the potato into a bowl, add the chopped green vegetables and the seasoning and mix well together. TASTE to see if there is enough salt and add more if it needs it. Press the mix well down into the pan, cover and fry over a low heat for about 10 minutes. Slice across into quarters and carefully turn each slice to brown the other side. Serve hot.

TIMELY TIPS

● It makes a difference frying this dish in a heavy pan with butter and garlic. If you can't spare that much butter then make it 1:1 with margarine or olive oil; the latter gives a Continental taste.

● The green vegetables need not be cooked; just shred them very fine and fry for a little longer.

★ *VARIATIONS* ★

★ Serve each slice topped with a fried egg and a little chopped grilled bacon. (Give 'em a slice each if you have enough.)

★ When you've turned the slices over, sprinkle the top with grated cheese and/or breadcrumbs, and after browning the underside put the pan under the grill to brown the top.

★ Experiment with the seasoning. Try a good dash of ginger instead of the bayleaf. If you're using olive oil to fry, add Herbes de Provence along with the bayleaf for a herby taste.

★ Grate a little lemon rind in with the first mixing – about ½ tsp per person – and don't forget the pepper.

POTATO BASE PIZZA

WHAT YOU NEED
(per person)

Potato ½ cup, mashed
Tomato ½
Cheese ¼ cup, grated
Seasoning
Basil, tarragon or chilli seasoning mix, ground pepper, salt

WHAT YOU DO

Use instant mashed potato mix made up fairly dry or the real thing if you saved some from yesterday, but it must be dry or it'll fall apart. If, on examination, yesterday's mash looks a little sloppy, stir in a tablespoon of brown flour or bran and mix well to help bind the potato.

In a heavy pan oiled with a little fat spread out the mash to form the base of the pizza and firm well down. Cook uncovered over the lowest heat you can manage for about 15 minutes till the bottom is well browned. Spread with sliced tomatoes and some grated cheese and cook covered for a further 7–8 minutes until the cheese melts, or finish off under the grill.

★ *VARIATIONS* ★

Using mashed potato as a base you can top it with anything you like. Try:

★ Pilchards mashed with a little lemon juice, a sprinkle of dill weed and topped with tomato slices. Grill until the tomatoes are done.

★ Mix chopped cooked bacon or garlic sausage and chopped leftover vegetables seasoned with oregano and garlic salt. Spread over the mash and top with a little grated cheese. Cook covered with a tight lid for 5–10 minutes. Grill to brown or sprinkle generously with paprika or Crunchy Topping.

★ Swish chopped mushrooms in a little milk to wet them before pressing them into the potato base. Sprinkle with tarragon and lay very thinly sliced tomato and onion over the top and give a brief dash of salt. Drizzle a little melted butter, margarine or olive oil over the top and grill until the onions are browned.

HASH BROWNS

An old American favourite, this.

WHAT YOU NEED
(for 2)

Potatoes 1 large
Egg 1
Brown flour 2 tsps
Fat or **Oil** for frying
Seasoning
Salt, Pepper

WHAT YOU DO

Grate the potato and blot away excess moisture with kitchen paper. Toss into a bowl with a well beaten egg and the brown flour. Mix well and drop spoonfuls of the mix into hot fat, pressing down the potatoes to help them stay together. Cook to golden brown on both sides. Put into a dish to keep warm while you cook the rest, sprinkling each batch with salt (to keep them crisp) and ground pepper.

STUNCH

Pronounce the 'u' as the 'oo' in good. This recipe I stole from my mother, but I don't know from whom she stole it. It could be a classic from somewhere up North, so if you recognise it or know it's origins I'd be interested to hear as it's new to everyone who eats it Bateau Moi.

WHAT YOU NEED
(per person)

Potatoes 1 medium
Carrots $\frac{1}{4}$ cup
Butter 1 tbsp
Milk $\frac{1}{8}$ cup
Seasoning
Salt $\frac{1}{8}$ tsp
Sugar $\frac{1}{8}$ tsp
Pepper 1 tsp

WHAT YOU DO

Cook the potatoes and carrots until tender. If you coarse grate the carrot it will cook in the same time as the potato chopped small. Drain well and stir to allow as much steam to escape as possible – wet mashed potato is the pits. Whilst still hot, mash the two vegetables to a fine texture, add a generous dollop of butter – about 1 tablespoon per person. Add $\frac{1}{8}$ teaspoon of salt and the same of sugar per person and LOADS of freshly ground pepper. Add a little milk but not enough to make the mix sloppy and beat all together furiously to distribute the seasoning. Serve as an accompaniment to your main course or as a dish in its own right.

Choose potatoes that cook fluffy not waxy; the good old King Edward potato, if you can get it, is still one of the best for mashing. This recipe does not work so well with new potatoes. Some people like the carrot in whole bits, so you needn't worry if the carrot is undercooked.

BOMBAY POTATOES

Another classic from the days of the Raj that you can serve with hot or cold meats, Lentil Loaf or even cold with a salad.

WHAT YOU NEED
(for 4)

Oil   3–4 tbsp
Onion   1 medium, sliced
Garlic   1 clove crushed or 1 tsp purée or granules
Potatoes   4 cups, cooked rough chopped
Seasoning
Curry powder   1 tbsp
Cumin seeds   1 tbsp
Mustard seeds   1 tbsp

WHAT YOU DO

Heat the oil in a heavy pan and gently fry the cumin and mustard seeds until they pop, then add the onion and garlic. Fry till golden brown, add the curry powder (or paste) and cook for another 2–3 minutes. Add the potatoes and turn in the pan to coat well with the curry mixture, adding a little water if the potatoes make it too dry. Taste and sprinkle on a little salt if necessary.

POTATO HAGGETY

WHAT YOU NEED
(per person)

Potatoes   1 medium
Onion   1 small
Oil   2 tbsp
Cheddar cheese $\frac{1}{2}$ cup, grated
Seasoning
Salt and fresh ground pepper   1 good pinch of each.
Cayenne pepper   1 pinch

WHAT YOU DO

Scrub but don't peel the potatoes. Slice as thinly as possible on 'Jaws' or with a sharp knife. Skin and slice the onion in rings. Heat the oil in your heaviest pan and when the bottom is nicely covered arrange the potatoes, onions and cheese in alternating layers, ending with cheese. Cover and allow to cook over a low heat for 15–20 minutes. As the potato softens press the whole lot down to amalgamate it all together. When the underside is brown turn the whole thing over and brown the other side (*see* Timely Tips). Serve in large slices with bacon or egg or both.

 *TIMELY TIPS*

● To turn the Haggety without breaking it up slide it out of the pan on to an oiled plate. Put another plate on top and invert the whole assembly; now you can slide the Haggety back into the pan to cook the other side. This leaves you with two dirty plates. You can either save them for serving (after all it's all the same dish) or slice the Haggety in the pan and turn a slice at a time. This is easier to do if you remove a slice first, turn the others then return the first slice, turned.

CANDIED POTATOES

This works equally well with yams and sweet potatoes.

WHAT YOU NEED
(per person)

Butter 1 tbsp
Orange juice 2 tbsp plus a few scraps of rind
Honey 1 tbsp
Potatoes ½ cup, cooked (new whole or old chopped)

WHAT YOU DO

Melt the butter and slowly add the juice, honey and rind. Heat until the mix simmers and then add the cooked potatoes, turning them to coat well. Cover and cook gently until the potatoes are heated through. Reduce the liquid by boiling rapidly if it's still too thin and pour over the served vegetables.

SPICED POTATOES

This goes one better than the last recipe. It takes a little longer but I think it's worth it if conditions allow.

WHAT YOU NEED
(for 3–4)

Potatoes 2 cups, raw (new whole or old chopped)
Onion 1 large
Garlic 1 clove or 1 tsp purée/granules
Root ginger 1 'toe' (about 1″ (25 mm))
Oil 2 tbsp
Butter 1 tbsp
Tomato purée 1 tbsp
Yoghurt (natural) 1 small pot (sheep's is best, then
                        goat's or cow's)
Honey 1 tsp, or brown sugar will do
Seasoning
Cumin 1 tsp
Caraway seeds 1 tsp
Salt and pepper 1 pinch of each

WHAT YOU DO

Put the potatoes on to cook, unpeeled, no salt. Peel and slice the onion, fresh garlic and ginger. Heat the oil and the butter in a heavy pan and cook the onion, garlic and ginger till tender. Add the cumin and caraway seeds and cook a further 2–3 minutes. Add the tomato purée, yoghurt and honey, stirring all the time. TASTE the sauce and add as much salt as you think it needs. Add the cooked drained potatoes and coat them with the sauce. Taste again and add pepper. Cook until potatoes are reheated (if they were cold) and serve.

 *TIMELY TIPS*

● You can effectively crush the ginger in the garlic press – and as both are going into the same dish you needn't wash it between uses.

POTATOES DI CALABRIA

I thought I'd invented this one when we were in Reggio di Calabria bouncing on the trampoline of a swell caused by the hydrofoil that periodically swept into the harbour with typical Italianate gusto. However, Maria in Cyprus said her mother had been making it for as long as anyone could remember and as Maria was no spring chicken at the time, this dish has been going around for ages. Don't skimp on the olive oil, garlic or parsley.

WHAT YOU NEED
(per person)

Potatoes   1 medium
Olive oil   1 tbsp
Garlic $\frac{1}{2}$ clove, crushed
Onion $\frac{1}{2}$ chopped small
Tomatoes $\frac{1}{2}$ cup (use a carton or (ssh!) a can)
Seasoning
Oregano $\frac{1}{2}$ tsp
Salt and pepper   Enough
Parsley   1 tbsp chopped (of the big leafed variety if you
          can get it)

WHAT YOU DO

Put the scrubbed but unpeeled potatoes (whole if new or rough chopped if old) to cook in plain water, no salt. Gently heat the olive oil in a large heavy pan, add the garlic and onion and cook till nearly tender. Add the tomatoes, oregano and half the parsley, mixing well so that the tomatoes break up to make a good sauce. TASTE and add enough salt to bring out the best in the tomatoes. Simmer the sauce until it thickens then add the drained, cooked potatoes and turn well to coat them. Cover and simmer till you're ready to serve. Cook uncovered to thicken the sauce further if you like. Sprinkle on the rest of the parsley, and add a good turn of the pepper mill on each serving.

★ *VARIATIONS* ★

★ If you add a generous topping of grated cheese and brown under the grill, or just allow it to melt in the covered pan and sprinkle with paprika, you have a complete meal.

★ If you really want to go to town you can stir in a beaten egg and cook gently until it firms up.

And now for Something Completely Different

Most people know how to cook the everyday vegetables, but it's worth trying some of the more 'un-English' ones that are now available, for a change. Here are some brief ideas if you haven't tried them already.

Yams, sweet potatoes and eddoes come from the Caribbean and sunny countries. Yams and sweet potatoes are about twice the size of the average ordinary potato. Yams have a rough brown skin. Peel them in water with salt and lemon juice as they darken quickly, and cook as you would ordinary potatoes; they have a nuttier flavour. Sweet potatoes have a smoother rosy skin with more eyes than ordinary potatoes and taste more like chestnuts. Peeled, then boiled or baked, the distinctive pink flesh is delightfully sweet. Try them parboiled and then baked with a little honey as a festive vegetable accompaniment to a roast. Eddoes are about potato size but very rough and hairy, quite comical really. Peel, boil with a little lemon juice to keep them white and mash with butter and a little grated nutmeg for a different taste.

Kohlrabi is a strange looking vegetable, like a cross between a turnip and a cabbage but sweeter. It is a member of the cabbage family but it is the centre stalk that swells to the size of an orange while the leaves remain vestigial on long stalks which are usually removed by the time we see them. It's a bit like spring cabbage to taste and worth a try. Cut them in half and boil until tender then scoop the flesh out of the skin and mash it with plenty of butter, salt and pepper. You can also use it finely grated, raw, in salad.

Mange tout and sugar snaps are both peas whose pods you eat as well. I feel cheated with mange tout because they are so thin, and much prefer the fatter sugar snap pea. Well named, it's delightful chopped raw in a salad or steamed for a minute or two (no longer) and rolled in butter and fresh ground pepper.

Aubergine is the glorious full plump and plum coloured fruit of the egg plant vine which, curiously, is part of the nightshade family. The skin is edible (no residue) and after wiping clean remove the stalk (well, hardly any residue) cut the aubergine into slices or cubes, sprinkle with salt and let sit for 20 minutes or so to allow the bitter juices to drain off. Blot with kitchen paper and fry gently in olive oil. Use in ratatouille, casseroles, and any tomato dish that needs something extra. Or bake it in two halves, allow to cool, then chop into cubes and serve with a yoghurt dressing. Or stuff with the lentil loaf mix (*see* Jane's Amazing Lentil Loaf p. 84) with added tomato paste and top with bread crumbs. Bake in a hot oven (425°F/220°C/GM7) for 30 minutes.

Celeriac is of the celery family and tastes the same but stronger and has a more solid texture. Peel and cube, boil and serve with butter and pepper or add to soups and casseroles where it will be the dominant flavour. It's a nice change raw in salads if shredded thinly with a squeeze of lemon.

Globe artichokes are a vastly overrated pastime to my mind, being merely a vehicle for the melted butter. I'll take the butter straight. But if you find yourself with a handful of these flower-like vegetables, have a go; they're very popular with the al fresco glitterati, I'm told. To cook, first soak them in cold water with a little lemon juice for 1 hour then trim the stem and make a cut across the top. Boil for about 30 minutes until you can pull the leaves off easily. Spread out the top and cut out the hairy 'choke' in the middle. Serve with garlic butter.

Mooli almost sounds like one of the late Kenneth William's jokes and looks like a huge white parsnip. It's from the radish family and has the same clean crisp taste. Grate it raw in salad or boil like a potato and serve with butter and freshly ground pepper. A good addition in chutney and pickles.

Baby sweetcorn I can see no point in eating. It seems a shame not to let them grow to full size when one will be enough for most people. As it is, each person needs three or four to get anything like a portion and they haven't had time to develop any flavour. Again, just a vehicle for melted butter but considered very 'posh' in some circles. Boil for about 5 minutes and use as a starter with the aforementioned butter, or chop in half and throw into a stir fry where you can make two halves do for one person.

Asparagus, would you believe, is part of the lily family and the fresh heads are as different from the tinned sort as it is possible to imagine. Considered a luxury in the UK because of the price, it is often a very cheap vegetable near Mediterranean shores. If your cruising takes you that way take the opportunity to gorge yourself while you have the chance. Boil the stalks lightly until tender (about 10 minutes) drain and serve with the good old melted butter or Hollandaise.

Avocado or alligator pear is the fruit of a West Indian tree, *Persea gratissima*. Prized for its rich creamy pale green flesh, the avocado is now cultivated in many parts of the world including Israel, South Africa and California. The fruit is ripe if it feels soft when gently pressed, though this must be done gently as the flesh bruises easily. Slice from pole to pole right through to the large slippery stone in the centre which should lift out easily if the fruit is properly ripe. The two halves can now be presented for eating with a small spoon and the addition of a vinaigrette or mayonnaise dressing.

Traditional base for a prawn hors d'œuvre, the flesh can also be scooped from the skin and used for dips or soup. This is a good wheeze when you discover the flesh is less than perfect. Mash the best bits with equal parts of yoghurt and a good pinch of ground bayleaf for a creamy dip or dressing. Carefully peeling the flesh allows you to slice it for salads or garnish, when one avocado can be spread among four people without too much hardship. Sprinkle with lemon juice if not to be eaten immediately to stop it discolouring. But I think it's great, straight.

Fennel looks a bit like an onion but with more top sprouts which are feathery. With its aniseed taste and smell it's not to everyone's liking, but boiled and mashed to a fine consistency with some cream it makes an unusual sauce; this is best done in a blender if you're ashore. It can add a piquancy to a green salad if finely grated raw, though it is an acquired taste, I think.

Salsify or oyster vegetable is very old fashioned, and was supposed to be a favourite with Elizabeth I. This long thin brown root is scraped then boiled with lemon juice to keep the flesh pale. Added to salad or served as a starter with a very thin butter sauce its delicate oyster-like flavour is a real conversation piece.

Squash is a term which, until recently in my mind at least, meant a fast and furious ball game or an over-sugary fruit drink. Now I know it also as a range of interesting and useful vegetables that are popular in America and are now available in the UK. Part of the marrow family, there's nothing wishy-washy about the following two bright yellow vegetables.

Butternut squash is a beige yellow with a keyhole shape. This squash has a lovely nutty taste and is much firmer than British marrow; the flesh is peachy coloured. Cut into large chunks and boil till tender then discard the skin. Mash the flesh with butter and season with practically anything, but add plenty of pepper. Used like marrow, it makes excellent jam and pickle.

Spaghetti squash is butter yellow in colour but shaped more like an ordinary marrow, but that's where the resemblance stops. Cut it in half lengthways – it's pretty hard so use a large sharp knife and wedge the squash on a roll of tea towel – and after scooping out the pips in the middle with a spoon, boil it in a large pan for about 30 minutes, though it's quicker to use the pressure cooker for about 10 minutes. Pull the flesh out by dragging a fork lengthways across the cooked part when it will come away like strands of spaghetti. Top with a nob of butter and a good turn of the pepper mill.

Plantain. This looks like an oversized green banana. Of the same family but with a milder flavour, it is cooked, after peeling, by frying pieces in butter or oil until soft and served as a vegetable. Plantains keep well and if left until the skins go brown have a sweeter flavour and can be fried as above but served with cream or a sprinkling of cinnamon sugar as a dessert. See also Grilled Bananas in the chapter on Desserts.

Other ideas

● Having thoughtfully cooked enough rice yesterday, you have some as a base for today's salad. Sprinkle a little ground cardamom and a squirt of lemon juice after adding the other ingredients to give a slightly oriental touch.

● Slow cook whole onions for sweetness. Serve as a vegetable in their own right. Thicken the cooking water as a sauce.

● Try rolling cooked rice in a little nut oil to keep it moist, if you think it might have to wait. Walnut and hazelnut oil are particularly tasty. The oil stops the rice gluing itself into clumps and, when cold, fries well with no additional fat.

● If your supermarket stocks the brown mushrooms, do give them a try. The white ones look so anaemic, while the brown are nuttier, seem to keep better and cost no more. Remember the days when you had to pay extra for brown eggs because the norm was white? You can't find a white egg for love nor money now; perhaps the same will happen to mushrooms.

Pressure cooking vegetables

If you already use a pressure cooker you will need no further encouragement from me. If, however, you still have reservations or a full size pressure cooker and think twice, as I did, each time you want to use it, give it a third thought. A pressure cooker can save you so much time, which means saving fuel and gives you more time to do other more interesting things. Get a small pressure cooker and give your large one to a friend.

To adapt cooking times for pressure cooking a rough rule of thumb is to allow one-third of the conventional cooking time. It is better to cook short and then do a little more than to over cook and end up with a mess; one minute too much can make all the difference.

One of the biggest advantages of the pressure cooker is that you can steam vegetables, thereby rendering them edible with the least loss of colour, flavour and nutrients – steamed new potatoes have to be tasted to be appreciated. I list below some cooking times, but be guided by the manufacturer's instructions.

Vegetables	Size	Approx. cooking time (mins)
Artichokes	Whole	10
Asparagus	Bunches	5
Green beans	Thick sliced	5
Broccoli	Single spears	2–3
Cabbage	Rough chopped	2
Carrots	$\frac{1}{4}''$ (6 mm) slices	4
Cauliflower	Small florets	2–3
Courgette	$\frac{1}{2}''$ (12 mm) slices	2

Vegetables	Size	Approx. cooking time (mins)
Marrow	1″ (25 mm) slices	3
Onion	Sliced	2 (5 if whole)
Parsnip	Slices, long	3–4
New potatoes	Small whole	5
Old potatoes	1″ (25 mm) cubes	4 (10 if whole)
Squash	Halves	10

Experiment with the cooking times; steaming vegetables as opposed to cooking them directly in the water takes a little longer. Also people's tastes differ and you may like your vegetables more, or less, cooked. The age of the vegetable is another consideration, as is the variety. Remember – always cook a little under rather than over and adjust to suit.

SPROUTING BEANS AFLOAT

Gardening in the galley is not as silly as you may think and is well worth doing for the sheer fun of being able to dish up crispy sprouts with a cry of 'Fresh from the garden!' Beans, when sprouted, increase their weight 10 times and their food value 100 fold or more and all on thin air and a twice daily rinse. They are full of protein, vitamins and will banish the scurvy, should you be so troubled. They will keep for a couple of days after harvesting, but it defeats the purpose of sprouting them if you don't use them immediately. Keep two jars going with successive planting, then you can have a continuous supply of fresh sprouts indefinitely. They require no cooking so strew them liberally in salads and sandwiches. In soups, casseroles, stir-frys and other hot dishes throw them in at the last moment and continue cooking only long enough to heat them through.

Mung beans or other (*see below*)

One or more 4 oz (100g) glass (or plastic) empty instant coffee jars.

Remove the card liner from inside the plastic cap and using a no. 8 bit in a hand-drill make at least 18 holes in the top of the lid. Clean off the swarf and you're ready to go.

Put 1 tablespoon of green mung beans in the jar, fill nearly to the top with fresh water and screw on lid. Allow to soak for an hour or two then invert the jar and allow to drain. Put the jar in a safe place somewhere in the galley, the darker the better. Rinse the sprouts twice daily allowing them to drain before putting them back into their storage. In 3–4 days, depending on temperature, you will have a jar full of fat, tasty sprouts ready for scattering raw over a salad or throwing into a stir fry.

Just about most beans will sprout, some taking a little longer than others. Most supermarkets, health shops and continental food stores stock a wide range. Mung beans seem to explode into jumbo sprouts and tiny alfalfa make a pale green nest of thread-fine sprouts. Brown lentils will sprout but pink lentils and split peas won't. If you're worried about eating raw beans because of that tricky enzyme, don't: it's converted in the sprouting process, rendering the raw sprout perfectly edible and nutritionally valuable. When the sprouts are nearly ready to eat, say a day short, put them in the light to green up a bit. A guide for types of bean, their sprouting times and approximate yields is given on page 120. If you have not tried sprouting beans before, give it a go ashore first.

Happy harvesting!

Francis Chichester grew mustard and cress on *Gypsy Moth IV* but decided that the crop was easier to harvest if grown on damp kitchen paper than when grown in earth.

Seeds	Sow	Yield	Days	Length	Goodies
Alfalfa	2 tsp	2 cups	4–5	1″	Tops for protein, minerals and vitamins A, B complex, C, D, E, K.
Mung	$\frac{1}{4}$ cup	2 cups	3–5	2″	Protein, vitamins A, C, calcium, phosphorus, iron.
Soy	$\frac{1}{2}$ cup	2 cups	4–6	1″	Complete protein, vitamins A, B complex, C, E.
Lentils	$\frac{1}{4}$ cup	2 cups	3–4	$\frac{1}{2}$″	Complete protein, vitamin B complex.
Wheat	$\frac{1}{2}$ cup	2 cups	2–7	$\frac{1}{4}$–1″	Good protein, vitamin B complex, C, E.

COOKING DRIED BEANS

(the easy way)

By and large, 1 cup of dried mixed beans will yield 2 cups of cooked beans (or four servings). So you can gauge quantities since the dried product will be twice the size when cooked. Cooking times vary according to the type of bean, so if you have a mix you must obviously time for the longest cooking bean (the shorter cooking bean will have to take its chance). Cooking beans by boiling them in water means they all jiggle about together rubbing shoulders with one another and generally getting in a mess. In the mixed bean scenario this means the smaller quicker bean ends up a mush, the middle cooking bean ends up with his jacket roughed up or torn off altogether and only the big bean looks in control. Fine if you want soup but the resultant mess can be a little offputting. This is where the pressure cooker comes to the rescue.

I have developed the following method of cooking beans to retain their shape, even with a varied mix, and you will find that your beans and pulses stay nicely separate and retain their colour. I have not seen this method mentioned in any recipe book, so just remember – you read it here FIRST!

WHAT YOU NEED
(for 3–4)

Dried beans   1 cup of your choice, pre-soaked
                  (see below)
Water   4 cups (boil the kettle, it's quicker)

WHAT YOU DO

Rinse the beans and place in the basket on the trivet in the pressure cooker. Pour over 4 cups of boiling water. Close lid of pressure cooker and bring to pressure quickly. When cooking pressure is reached, adjust heat to the lowest without dropping pressure, and time as below. Release steam, open the lid and examine the largest bean for doneness. If in doubt replace lid and cook for another few minutes at full pressure.

 *TIMELY TIPS*

● When releasing pressure or removing lid, stand back as the steam rising from the pan can scald – or fog your glasses.
● The basket must be clear of the pan base and the water level. These beans are cooking in steam, so if your basket is flat bottomed and you don't have a trivet, stand it on a couple of spoons.

SOAKING PROCEDURES

All dried pulses (that includes beans, peas, etc.) should be soaked before cooking, with the exception of red lentils, though even they benefit from a short (1 hour) soak. The soaking starts the rehydration process and, more essentially, helps to make the bean more digestible and less 'gassy'. This soaking can be done two ways.

1. If you've got your act together the night before, just sling enough dried beans/pulses in a tall vessel and cover to twice their depth in water – plain, not salt – and let them stand till morning. Drain, rinse and cook in fresh water.

2. Panic strikes and it's already mid-afternoon. Just sling the required amount of beans/pulses into a tall vessel and cover with twice their height in BOILING water and let them stand for 2 hours before draining, rinsing and cooking. If it occurs to you during the soak time, you can drain them, and cover again with fresh boiling water and leave till you're ready to cook, but once will do. I use the boiling water method even for the long soak as I reckon it improves the digestibility.

COOKING TIMES FOR 1 CUP DRY MEASURE

Pulse	Time from FULL pressure (mins)
Adzuki beans	10
Butter beans	15
Black-eyed beans	15
Chick-peas	35
Dried whole peas	40
English field beans	15
Haricot beans	15
Red lentils	1, or just to pressure only
Mixed beans	25
Red kidney beans	15 MINIMUM, even if less than 1 cup
Split peas	8
Soya beans	25

Cooking times for beans seem to vary from batch to batch. I think it may be something to do with the time since harvest and the method of storage, or a combination of both and other factors. You will have to experiment and find out for yourself. The advantage with my basket method of cooking is that a little extra time will not render the beans a soggy mass, though one or two may burst their jackets.

Lentils take such a short time to cook it's hardly worth using the pressure cooker, unless of course, you are adding lentils as part of the recipe as in Five Minute Soup (*see* chapter on Soups).

A reminder – As mentioned in the chapter Victualling, some dried beans (mainly the red kidney bean and similar) contain an enzyme which can upset the stomach if it is not cooked out. What this means in simple terms is that the beans, after soaking, must be cooked at a vigorous boil for 10 minutes before lowering the heat under the pan to continue cooking at a simmer. The enzyme is rendered harmless at temperatures above 200°F (98°C), hence the need to cook at a rolling boil for 10 minutes. The problem is easily overcome, however, by using a pressure cooker because all cooking is done at temperatures in excess of boiling point.

DESERT ISLAND DESSERTS

Desserts don't get dished every night on most craft; it's more likely to be a 'bought' dessert or yoghurt, a piece of fruit or a slice of cake and a cup of tea. But there are occasions when you will want to produce something different so here are some ideas. They are all easy, popular and quite un-sensational. The first is one of my favourites.

DIB'S LEMMING SURPRISE PUDDING

WHAT YOU NEED
(for 4)

Eggs   2
Lemon   1 large or two small
Sugar $\frac{1}{2}$ cup
SR flour $\frac{2}{3}$ cup brown or white
Margarine $\frac{1}{4}$ cup
Milk $1\frac{1}{3}$ cup

WHAT YOU DO

Separate the egg whites into a $3\frac{1}{2}$-pint (2-litre) jug or other tall vessel. Whisk till stiff. Turn into cooking container (oven-glass soufflé bowl or cake tin, preferably non-stick) and set aside. Back to that jug (and whisk), unwashed. Into it squeeze the juice from the lemon, add the egg yolks and all the other ingredients – except the milk – and whisk hard to mix. Add milk and whisk again then tip the lot over the egg whites and blend gently. Bake in a hot oven (425°F/220°C/GM7) for 40–45 minutes. The top should look like a golden brown sponge with a crazed surface revealing the lemony goo underneath.

★ *VARIATIONS* ★

★ Try adding a little vanilla essence and/or chopped nuts. Most soft fruit works in place of lemon as long as it's pulped, though lemon still remains the best.

★ Use honey instead of sugar if you are allergic or just for the hell of it.

★ Replace a tablespoon of milk with rum or brandy in the lemon mix for a more exotic flavour.

TIMELY TIPS

● If you're ashore put the egg/lemon etc. through the blender.

● Scrape the flesh from the lemon after squeezing and grate a little of the rind; add both to the mix. This gives little surprises in the middle of the sponge.

● Use one of the measuring cups to hold the two yolks while you whisk the whites; if using one egg for a two-person pudding leave the yolk sitting in the separator.

● Use a spatula for sweeping most of the egg white out of the jug so that you can use the jug, unwashed, for mixing the rest of the ingredients. The final mix in the cooking container is done gently so as not to lose too much of the air from the egg whites.

● The margarine blends more easily if it's gently warmed in one of your nice little stainless cups held over a low burner, cup of coffee, the engine or a cigarette lighter.

● Finally, if you really can't face separating the egg whites just throw the whole lot in together and give it a jolly good whisking till frothy. It will still come out pretty tasty, if not so fluffy.

● Non-stick cookware makes for easier washing up.

● Remember, egg whites will not whisk if contaminated by the slightest hint of yolk or grease, so always whisk the whites first.

MISER'S INSTANT MUESLI

If you're stuck with only one fruit, say apples, try the following recipe. One apple does two people – a real Econo-Dessert.

WHAT YOU NEED
(for 2)

Rolled oats   ½ cup
Apple   1
Seasoning
Cardamom   1 pinch, ground, not seeds

WHAT YOU DO

Put the rolled oats into a bowl and mix in the ground cardamom. Wash but don't peel the apple, just remove any obvious bruising or scars. Chop it small with 'Jaws' or a sharp knife or grate coarsely. Mix into the rolled oats thoroughly, divide in two equal portions and serve immediately.

★ *VARIATIONS* ★

★ I like it just like that, but if you think it's too dry then use carton fruit juice, or fruit squash neat or made up 1:1 with water (1 to 2 tablespoons per person). The cardamom gives an unusual lift and the rolled oats provide just enough bulk to satisfy.

FRIED BANANAS

WHAT YOU NEED
(per person)

Bananas   1 (unpeeled)
Butter or oil   1 tbsp

WHAT YOU DO

Heat the butter or oil gently in a heavy pan. Lay the unpeeled bananas in the hot fat and fry very gently, turning occasionally until the skins are black all over. Lift on to a plate and strip off the skin along the top of the banana and serve. The flesh is scooped out with a spoon.

★ Sprinkle with cinnamon sugar or a drizzle of honey, maple/
golden syrup or malt extract. Top with a glob of icecream/cream/
evaporated milk.

★ Bananas can also be grilled or cooked over a barbeque.

BASIC PANCAKE BATTER

(Does for Yorkshire Puddings too, if you've a mind.)

Don't forget the simple pancake. The batter can be made
ahead of time and stored in a sealed container in a cool place or
fridge (the batter improves with cooling after mixing). Pancakes
can be cooked ahead of time and stored one on top of the other.
Later just peel off each one and set it back in the pan, add the
filling, fold up into a parcel and put it in a warm oven. Fillings can
be from a spoonful of jam to exotic fruits and liqueurs. They can
also be savoury, where a little filling goes a long way.

WHAT YOU NEED
(makes 6–8 pancakes)

Egg   1
Plain flour   1 cup
Salt   Just a pinch
Milk   1+cup

WHAT YOU DO

Drop the egg into the flour and salt – you can sift the flour first if
you're keen – and start to mix it in, gradually adding the milk to
form a smooth batter. Whisk well to make sure there are no lumps
and set aside in a cool place for an hour if possible.

Heat a little oil in a heavy pan over a medium heat and pour in
$\frac{1}{4}$ cup of batter, tipping the pan to spread the batter all round.
Cook uncovered until the surface of the pancake goes dull and
little holes appear. Lift with a spatula or fish slice and turn to
cook the other side.

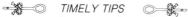   *TIMELY TIPS*

● For a richer batter use 2 eggs or for a lighter batter use half
water to milk – iced water if you have it.

● Adding a little oil to the batter mix can help prevent sticking if
you don't have a non-stick pan.

● Add 1 teaspoon ground ginger (more or less according to
taste) to the flour before mixing. The pancakes are nice plain with

the usual sprinkle of sugar and lemon juice or use with some of the sweet or savoury fillings suggested below for something different.

● After mixing the egg into the flour add just enough liquid to make a stiff batter and allow to stand for a half hour, if you have the time, then beat in the rest of the liquid. This allows any small lumps to dissolve.

● Pancake batter benefits from resting in a cool place and will keep for a day or two in a fridge. Whisk again before using.

FILLINGS

Put the filling on the cooked side of the pancake after turning and when the underside is done either roll up in the traditional way or make a parcel. Parcels are best with bulky vegetable fillings with a lot of juice. Pancakes cooked ahead of time can be kept warm uncovered in a low oven. Sprinkle the sweet pancakes with sugar and a squeeze of lemon. Dust savoury ones with a little salt.

SWEET FILLINGS:

● Jams of all sorts
● Mincemeat
● Rough-chopped bananas sprinkled with cinnamon sugar
● Fresh fruit chopped very fine
● Cream cheese with chopped pineapple or orange
● As above but with nuts as well
● Gibstruedl (*see* opposite)
● Wheatgerm, oatmeal and dried fruit mixed with honey – highly nutritious

SAVOURY FILLINGS:

● Mashed tuna and mayonnaise, plenty of pepper
● Mashed potato and cheese, abundant pepper
● Cooked rice, anchovies, chopped tomato, liberal pepper
● Chopped cooked vegetables, grated cheese, generous pepper
● Chopped mushrooms rolled in garlic butter, plethora of pepper
● Grated cheese, chopped tomato, dill weed, dusting of pepper
● Cooked rice, chopped garlic sausage or bacon, no pepper
● Cooked shrimps, Thousand Mud-Flat Dressing, tiny bit of pepper
● Flaked cooked fish, butter, lemon, parsley, sprinkle of pepper

GIBSTRUEDL

This is a filling for open or closed tarts, pancakes and muesli biscuits.

WHAT YOU NEED
(to fill 6 pancakes)

Mincemeat   ½ cup
Brown breadcrumbs   1 cup
Honey   2 tbsp
Seasoning
Cinnamon   1 tsp

WHAT YOU DO

Mix all ingredients until the breadcrumbs have soaked up the juice. Use a spoonful in pancakes or in plain pastry tartlets. Or make struedl using ready-made flaky pastry.

★ *VARIATIONS* ★

★ Try using it as a filling between two layers of the Muesli Biscuit mixture (see page 156) , adding a little more honey or hot water to make it easier to spread. Bake.

★ Substitute golden syrup for the honey, press the mix into a pastry case and bake for 30 minutes in a hot oven (425°F/220°C/GM7) for a treacle tart with a difference.

★ Substitute malt extract if you don't have or like honey.

★ Add a drop of the hard stuff to the mix to ward off the plague.

GILLIE'S RUM CREAM

WHAT YOU NEED
(for 4–6)

Egg yolks   3
Castor sugar   4 tbsp
Rum   2 tbsp (or more according to taste)
Double cream   ½ cup

WHAT YOU DO

Whisk the egg yolks and sugar until thick and frothy. Add rum (allowing the customary tot for the cook). Whisk cream until thick and fold into egg mixture. Serve in small dishes topped with chopped nuts.

YOGHURT

Don't back off – yoghurt is child's play to make and the home-made sort is sweeter, tastier, fresher and cheaper than the commercial kind. All you need is a spoonful of live yoghurt to start you off, thereafter the process is self-perpetuating – as long as you remember not to gobble the last spoonful but save it to start the next batch.

WHAT YOU NEED

Milk   3 cups any sort, liquid or dried
Starter   1 tsp of live yoghurt or previous batch

WHAT TO DO

Heat the milk very gently but don't let it boil, just keep it at a low simmer for 4–5 minutes. Allow to cool to just hand hot. Put the 'starter' in a wide-mouthed insulated flask or the yoghurt-maker mentioned in the Galley chapter and mix with 1 tablespoon of the warm milk. Mix thoroughly till it is creamy with no lumps and gradually add the rest of the warm milk, stirring to make sure the 'starter' is well blended. Cap the flask/yoghurt maker and put it in a quiet spot for 5–6 hours and the yoghurt is made. Enjoy.

 TIMELY TIPS

● The milk turns into yoghurt by bacterial action. It is heated to just under boiling point to destroy other bacteria that would interfere with the process. Remember to cool the simmered milk to 'hand hot' so as not to kill the working bacteria.

● Any milk can be used as long as it is simmered first, with the exception of goat's milk which must not boil. The richer the milk the richer the yoghurt. If you want the Queen of Yoghurts blend in a tub of single or double cream with the 'starter' and heat slowly to just boiling point but do not simmer. Evaporated milk added to the standard mix will also enrich the flavour.

● Once made you can add your own flavourings with fresh fruit, honey or fruit syrups.

● Only use plain yoghurt as your 'starter' for the next batch.

★ *VARIATIONS* ★

★ To make a delightful light cheese, turn the yoghurt out into a fine mesh sieve and suspend over a pan to catch the whey. Leave for about 8 hours, or longer if you want a firmer cheese. Add crushed garlic or garlic granules, finely chopped onion or chives, pimento or celery, parsely or other herbs. Any of the seasoned pepper mixes add a nice bite. Dill weed with poppy seeds is different.

★ TASTE and add salt as you think fit.

★ This cheese is lovely with finely chopped citrus fruit or pineapple, sitting on crackers for a snack. Or try Aunt Janet's Easy Cheesecake, after the next recipe.

JAMAICAN YOGHURT

Still got some bananas that are running around by themselves? Try this quick dessert; it goes down well after a curry or Pepper Pot Mushrooms.

WHAT YOU NEED
(per person)

Bananas 1 unless they are very large, then $\frac{1}{2}$
  (the riper the better)
Yoghurt $\frac{3}{4}$ cup or a 4 oz (100 g) carton
Seasoning
Ginger $\frac{1}{2}$ tsp grated fresh or $\frac{1}{8}$ tsp dried

WHAT YOU DO

Mash bananas with the grated/dried ginger till well blended. Add the yoghurt and swirl around till nearly mixed (the swirls look attractive and they can always mix it more if they want). Garnish with sugar strands or flaked almonds or Crunchy Topping.

AUNT JANET'S EASY CHEESECAKE

Janet sailed away to the Caribbean with a sea captain from Boston and hasn't been heard of since; the following is her only legacy to me.

WHAT YOU NEED
(for 4–6)

Biscuit crust
Digestive biscuits   10, crushed to crumbs
Butter $\frac{1}{3}$ cup
Filling
Gelatine   1 tbsp of dried granules
Egg yolks   2
Honey $\frac{1}{4}$ cup, clear
Cream cheese   2 cups, your own yoghurt cheese
                   or any other
Lemon juice   2 lemons squeezed, plus some shreds
                  of rind
Double cream $\frac{1}{2}$ cup

WHAT YOU DO

Put the gelatine granules along with 3 tablespoons of cold water in one of your measuring cups and stand it in a mug of boiling water; leave to dissolve. Meanwhile make the crumb crust by melting the butter and folding in the biscuit crumbs until all is absorbed. Press into a 7–8″ (18–20 cm) pie tin, smooth down with the back of a metal spoon and put in a cool place to set. Have a look at the gelatine; stir it, and if it hasn't dissolved set it over more boiling water.

Make the filling by blending the egg yolks, honey and cheese with the pump whisk, or a blender. Stir in the lemon juice, shreds of peel and gelatine, whisking again to make sure all the ingredients are well mixed. Whisk the double cream till floppy and add to the cheese/lemon mixture – whisk again just enough to blend. Pour the mixture on to the biscuit base and smooth over. Decorate with the last few shreds of lemon rind or some grated chocolate. Put in a cool place to set.

CHOCOLATE BRANDY MOUSSE

Mousse used to be another of those 'mysteries' that looked so exotic but are, once you've tried them, simplicity themselves. Almost anything can be made into a mousse and it's not restricted to sweet things.

WHAT YOU NEED
(for 4)

Plain chocolate 1 bar (4 oz (100 g) size)
Coffee 2 tbsp, strong black or ½ tsp instant coffee powder
Brandy 1 tbsp (don't ask him – take it)
Eggs 3 separated
Whipping cream 1 small tub/tin/carton
Chocolate strands Enough to decorate

WHAT YOU DO

Break the chocolate into small pieces and set to melt in a small pan over a larger pan of hot, but not boiling, water. When the chocolate has melted, carefully stir in the coffee and the brandy. Break up the egg yolks and add to the chocolate through a sieve or tea strainer to get rid of any stringy bits, stirring well to blend; leave the mixture to cool. Meanwhile, whisk the egg white until very stiff and fold into the COOL chocolate mixture. Pour into serving dishes and put in a cool place to set for at least 1 hour. Decorate with whipped cream and chocolate strands.

TIMELY TIPS

● Never let the chocolate get too hot or it goes grainy, although adding a little vegetable oil will sometimes save a grainy mix. Use vegetable oil for thinning also. Remember, chocolate is a fat so never use water to thin it.
● If you have no cool place and the weather is warm the mousse might not set too well. Here's what you do. Put 1 tablespoon of gelatine granules into the cold water for the coffee, which you add as Instant when the gelatine has melted and the water is heated. The gelatine should hold the lot together in all but blistering heat. In which case you wouldn't be making it anyway.

★ *VARIATIONS* ★

★ If you have any exotic liqueurs try them instead of the brandy. Creme de Cacao is addictive, and Benedictine is not too dusty either. I'll leave you to discover other decadencies.
★ Pour over evaporated milk if you haven't got cream.

FRUIT AND HONEY PASTA

Apart from the obvious milk pudding type of sweet pasta which is not too easy afloat and not everyone's favourite ashore, you can rush up a quick dessert with any sort of plain pasta you might have left over from a previous meal. If you're short on fruit this helps to eke it out.

WHAT YOU NEED
(for 4)

Cooked plain pasta 2 cups
Fruit 1 cup chopped fruit, anything
Honey $\frac{1}{3}$ cup
Lemon juice About half a lemon, squeezed
Arrowroot 1 tbsp or cornflour
Water 1 cup
Seasoning
Cinnamon, cloves or ginger $\frac{1}{2}$ tsp of whichever is
most suitable to the fruit
you're using

WHAT YOU DO

Mix the fruit with the cooked pasta gently so as not to break up the pasta. In a small pan or your largest metal measuring cup gently heat the honey, lemon juice and chosen spices. Mix the arrowroot with a little water, add to the honey mixture and cook gently until it is thickened and clear. Pour over the fruit/pasta mix and turn so that all the pieces are covered.

★ *VARIATIONS* ★

★ Never forget the alcohol. This is another little dish that takes well to a splash from the Skipper's Cabinet.
★ If you're still short on quantity throw in a handful of dried mixed fruit to the warming juice and allow to swell.
★ Grapes and slices of banana are nice together.

Things that you might not otherwise attempt to cook afloat can be made quite easily in the pressure cooker. Try the following puddings and see if you agree.

LEN'S EGG CUSTARD

Uncle Len never sails anywhere; this guy flies or he doesn't go. He taught me to make this in the oven – 2 hours at (200°F/100°C/ GM½) works just fine ashore, but I've adapted it for the pressure cooker to work afloat.

WHAT YOU NEED
(for 2)

Milk   2 cups
Eggs   1
Sugar   1 tbsp
Seasoning
Vanilla   A couple of drops
Nutmeg   Enough to grate over the top

WHAT YOU DO

Warm the milk gently in a pan. Meanwhile beat the eggs, vanilla and sugar in an oven-proof bowl and pour on the warmed milk. Sprinkle on the nutmeg and cover the bowl with greaseproof paper secured with string. Stand the covered bowl on the trivet in the cooker and add 2 cups of water. Close the lid, bring to full pressure and cook for 7 minutes. Release steam slowly.

TIMELY TIPS

● You can strain the mix into the bowl to get rid of the stringy egg bits if you like, though they never seem to appear if you don't. One more thing to wash up, though.

★ *VARIATIONS* ★

★ Use 2 eggs and/or evaporated milk for a richer pudding.

CHESTNUT DELIGHT

I used a can of chestnut purée for this and it worked well, though the purists among you can cook and peel fresh chestnuts if you want to. A small dish of this rich dessert is enough for most people.

WHAT YOU NEED
(for 4–6)

Sugar $\frac{1}{3}$ cup
Water   2 cups
Chestnut purée   2 cups, or 1 × 1 lb (450 g) tin
Butter $\frac{1}{3}$ cup
Eggs   4 separated
Seasoning
Vanilla   A few drops

WHAT YOU DO

Boil the sugar in the water to make a light syrup, adding the vanilla. Mix the chestnut purée into the syrup and add the butter, stirring to mix well. Leave to cool a little before adding the lightly whisked egg yolks. Whisk the whites till 'peaky' and carefully fold into the chestnut mix. Turn the whole lot into a non-stick straight-sided soufflé dish and cover with greaseproof paper secured with string. Stand the dish on the trivet, adding 2 cups of boiling water and cook at full pressure for 20 minutes. Release steam slowly and remove the dish, allowing the pudding to cool before turning out onto a plate. Decorate with grated chocolate or a squirt from a spray can of cream.

★ *VARIATIONS* ★

★ I like it without the chocolate but with vanilla ice cream or evaporated milk.

FRUIT SALAD

Fruit salads are the sea cook's stand by for dessert, but some think it's very boring. Here are some ideas to lift the fruit salad out of the ordinary.

● Don't peel the apples, just wash the skin well. The contrast of the peel looks nice; besides, the vitamins are in the skin.

• Hate peeling oranges for a fruit salad? Try this method. Slice the orange through the equator, then slice each half through the pole and again on a Great Circle. Hold a wedge thus made in one hand and slide your sharp knife between the flesh and the pith with the other, pressing the blade down on the board to flatten the peel. Cut the resultant crescent into pieces. Repeat with the other segments. This effectively removes the peel but you might have a little flesh left on the inside, so just bend the newly severed peel over the knife and squeeze the juice into the bowl. This works best with a large wide 2″ (5 cm) bladed knife which flattens the skin so effectively there is seldom much flesh left behind.

• In a small pan or the largest of your stainless steel measuring cups put the juice from the orange. If you have no juice use $\frac{1}{2}$ cup water, stir in $\frac{1}{8}$ cup honey, malt extract, golden syrup or brown sugar. While no one's looking, slosh in a good nip (tablespoon) of the Skipper's brandy, sherry or port or try Dubonnet. Blend in $\frac{1}{2}$ teaspoon of arrowroot and heat very gently to thicken. Pour over the fruit salad and mix well.

• If that's too much trouble, try some rosewater (available from any chemist) mixed with the natural juice of the fruit, or just sprinkled over the top of the chopped fruit. This makes a fragrant dessert that has most people guessing. (It's also lovely to put on tired eyes with cotton wool; comb a little through your hair and add to the rinse water of your undies. Mixed 1:1 with glycerine it's a soothing skin balm for sunburn, or with honey for eczema.)

• Failing rosewater, try just a little Angostura Bitters. Now you must have that; no self-respecting skipper would sail without the Bitters – how else do you Pink your Gin once the sun is over the yard-arm?

• Dried mixed fruit should be allowed to swell in a little water (dull), orange juice (better), alcohol (best) before adding to the salad if the fresh fruit is limited. Even plain old apples come up looking and tasting great, chopped on 'Jaws' and bulked out with the swelled mixed fruit. If you have mint, sprinkle a little on top, finely chopped with scissors.

• Almost any fresh fruit can be improved with the addition of a simple libation made like this: Take 1 tablespoon of port, the same of undiluted orange squash or juice, double the amount with water and mix. Pour over chopped or sliced fruit. These quantities are enough to cover sliced pears for 4 people, for instance. Try adding a pinch of cinnamon/mixed spice, or with apple, ground cloves. If you like it sweeter add 1 teaspoonful of honey.

With this liquid you can use up fruit that is a little past its best, peeling and cutting out bruised parts and slicing the remainder.

Throw over a little dried mixed fruit or chopped glacé cherries to jazz it up a bit or to bulk it out if you're short on quantity. You can also add medium rolled oats to make the dish a little more filling – try about 1 tablespoon per person.

● One apple chopped fine or julienne'd on 'Jaws' plus 1 tablespoon of dried mixed fruit and a slurp of the above cocktail will make an agreeable dessert for 2 people.

SUMMER PUDDING

This dish is as old as the hills but it's easy to make and can be left to cool and set till needed. Any stewed fruit will do, but the addition of the soft summer fruits like raspberries, strawberries or cherries give it its typical rich colour. It's cheap (sorry, economical) too. Tinned pie fillings work well but need a little extra fluid.

WHAT YOU NEED
(for 4)

Gelatine $\frac{1}{2}$ tbsp, granules
Bread 4–5 slices with crusts removed
Stewed fruit 2 cups plus 1 cup of juice

WHAT YOU DO

Put the gelatine granules into $\frac{1}{2}$ cup of liquid from the fruit and set over a very gentle heat to melt. (A metal measuring cup sitting on top of a mug of boiling water works fine.) Line the bottom and sides of a pudding basin with the bread. When the gelatine has dissolved completely, mix it into the stewed fruit – saving a little of the juice – then pour the fruit into the bread-lined basin, pressing it down with the back of the spoon. Cover the top with more bread, tucking the edges well down and pour over the juice to soak the bread. Put a saucer over the bread and weigh it down with something heavy to compress the pudding. Leave for at least 4 hours. Serve with anything sweet that pours.

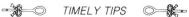 *TIMELY TIPS*

● White bread or light brown bread work best. Cut the crusts off but don't be too fussy about trimming the slices to fit the bowl, just let them overlap each other.

● If you're short on fruit, layer it with bread as you fill the basin but make sure there's plenty of juice to soak the bread.

● You can use a sponge cake (even one that's gone wrong) instead of bread.

● To stew fruit (apples, pears and soft fruit) simmer the washed, chopped fruit in a little water in closed pan until soft. Then add $\frac{1}{4}$ cup of sugar to each cup of prepared fruit and mix well. (Cooking fruit with sugar toughens the skins.) Thicken the juice with a little arrowroot mixed with cold water and stirred into hot fruit until it cooks clear.

● If using tinned pie filling, add 1 cup water.

BREAD, CAKES AND BISCUITS

Bread

There are very few mysteries in this life, I have found, that bear close investigation. What might appear, on the surface, to be a complex conundrum will often – with a little study – reveal its component parts to be mundane and within reach of all. Bread-making is one of these. It is so easy to make bread and I never knew. Bread-making also invests you with that Earth Mother aura; just casually mention that you always make your own bread and watch your credit level rise along with the eyebrows. If your luck's out there may be another Smart Article who will announce that she does too. In which case the pair of you can launch into a spirited discussion over the merits of various types of yeast; you can get good mileage out of that one too.

The Basic Bread recipe given here gets only one rising and is none the worse for that; the addition of Vitamin C speeds the rising process. You need to be around for about 2 hours to see the thing through but you're only actually doing something with it for 15 minutes or less, and even that is broken into two parts of 5 and 10 minutes. So it's a good excuse to hide away with that novel you wanted to finish.

'I can't possibly come now,' you call from the deep recesses of your bunk or wherever, 'I'm making bread.' No one will argue with that because they know the results are so good and as most people believe there are mystical rights involved with bread-making don't disabuse them of this impression.

If you can get fresh yeast, so much the better. Crumbly and with it's distinctive smell it adds to the intrigue. It makes little difference to the bread if you use dried yeast; just be caught apparently muttering incantations over it to keep your reputation intact. The Easy Blend type of dried yeast needs no frothing time and is mixed into the flour and water; the resultant dough is kneaded straight away. Ordinary dried yeast has proved very satisfactory and lasts for a good three months once the drum is opened. Push a little cushion of cling film down over the granules to exclude the air. If bought in sealed sachets dried yeast should keep for a year. Live yeast freezes well and I batch mine into $\frac{1}{4}$ cup packets wrapped in greaseproof paper, which are then stored in a small plastic container. Allow to thaw at room temperature and use as normal.

BASIC BREAD DOUGH

You can use this recipe with any sort of Bread Flour; brown, wholemeal or stoneground, white, granary or a mix. Try 2:1 white to brown if your crew are still addicted to white bread. They may hardly notice the difference at first and you can gradually increase the ratio. A 50:50 mix makes a nice light textured bread that toasts well.

WHAT YOU NEED
(makes 1 large loaf)

Yeast   2 tbsp fresh/1 tbsp granules
Warm water   1 cup
Salt and sugar $\frac{1}{4}$ tsp of each
Vitamin C   250 mg ($\frac{1}{2}$ a 500 mg tablet) crushed
Fat   2 tbsp (butter, margarine or oil)
Bread flour   3 cups

WHAT YOU DO

Crumble the fresh yeast into the warm water with the sugar and crushed Vitamin C. (For dried yeast follow the instructions on the packet and, after cutting in the fat, go straight to ★.) Cut the fat into the flour and salt with the pastry blender. At this stage, if you have access to a microwave, warm the flour for 25 seconds on full power. If not it doesn't matter, but try to keep bowl and environment warm. Tip the (fresh) yeast water into the flour but do not mix. Cover the bowl with a cloth to keep the warmth in and dive into your book for 15 minutes. When you come back the yeast should be frothing nicely in the flour.

★ Mix the whole lot together using a rubber spatula till it becomes a sticky dough and continue with the spatula for a minute or two until dry enough to handle. Then knead with gusto for about 10 minutes until it becomes smooth and elastic. Press the dough well down into a large loaf tin, non-stick or well-greased, cover with a cloth and set in a warm place out of drafts till risen to twice its size. (If the dough shows no signs of rising after 1 hour in a warm environment then either the yeast is dead (you killed it with too much heat) or it was too old. If everything is kept nicely warm the dough should start to rise within 10 minutes.) Bake in a hot oven (425°F/220°C/GM7) for 25–30 minutes.

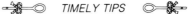 *TIMELY TIPS*

● Bread can be made from just about any flour but 'strong' flour is the best since it has a higher gluten content.

● The raising agent in bread, yeast, is activated by sugar, moisture and warmth. It releases CO_2 in little bubbles, held together by strands of gluten. This is what gives the bread its springy texture.

● Yeast likes warmth (100–110°F) (39–45°C) and sugar. It doesn't like salt or fat, or excessive heat or cold – the first three kill it and cold retards it. Yeast likes to be *fresh*.

● Kneading is the key to light springy bread. Unlike pastry where a light cool touch is essential, you really have to punch seven shades of hell out of the bread dough to make the gluten elastic. Roll, stretch, fold, and turn the dough until the imprint of your thumb rises back out as you watch.

● Many recipes specify covering the dough with oiled cling film or putting it in an oiled polythene bag. I have never gone to these complicated and messy lengths and the dough has never stuck to the cloth.

● The dough is risen enough when it gets to double the size you pressed into the pan, with a rounded top easing gently over the edges.

● The bread is cooked when, if you tip it out of the pan and rap your knuckle on its bottom like you might knock on a door, it sounds hollow. If it sounds a dull thud, pop it back without the tin, upside down and give it another 5 minutes or so. This extra cooking won't hurt the bread, it'll just be more crusty – which is better than being undercooked.

● Watch the barometer before starting a batch of yeast for bread. A quickly falling barometer nearly always spells disaster for my bread but you may be luckier. If the loaf comes out of the oven feeling heavy you know not enough water has been driven off and the bread will be stodgier. If toasting doesn't save it, turn it into Bread Pudding (*see* below).

★ *VARIATIONS* ★

★ Try other shapes. Roll into a long lozenge and slash the top diagonally with a sharp knife for a **Bloomer**.

★ Divide into three or four parts, roll out long and thin and plait, sealing both ends well.

★ For a **Cottage Loaf** roll unequal halves into balls, press the smaller on the larger and stab through the middle of both with the floured handle of a wooden spoon to cleave the parts together. (I don't have to tell you to remove the wooden spoon before baking do I?).

★ For **Rolls**, divide into pieces HALF the desired finished size, roll into balls and bake for 15 minutes. For a change, try rolling the pieces into sausage shapes and tying an overhand knot, or rolling it up like a snail. Make mini 'cottage' rolls. All these shapes are made BEFORE the dough is set to rise, and then baked on a tray when risen.

★ Brush the top of risen dough with milk for a nice brown finish (whoever beat up an egg just to glaze?). Sprinkle poppy seeds or a little salt on top of white rolls and rolled oats or sesame seeds on brown for a really professional effect.

BASIC BREAD PUDDING

This is a good recipe for any sort of bread you have left over.

WHAT YOU NEED
(for an 8-slice cake)

Bread   2 cups or 4 slices
Milk   1 cup or enough to mix
Dried fruit   1 cup
Butter $\frac{1}{2}$ cup
Sugar   1 cup
Golden syrup $\frac{1}{2}$ cup
Seasoning
Cinnamon   2 tsp
Mixed spice   1 tsp
Ginger   1 tsp ground or crushed root

WHAT YOU DO

Roughly chop the bread into small cubes; place in a large bowl and pour the milk over. Press the bread into the milk with a saucer and leave to absorb while you find and measure out the rest of the ingredients. Add them to the soaked bread and mix thoroughly, turn into a greased cake tin and bake for 45 minutes in a hot oven (425°F/220°C/GM7).

TIMELY TIPS

● If you can give the bread an hour or so to soak up the milk, it helps; if not throw all the other ingredients into the bowl and mix well.

● If the mix is reluctant to hold together (know the feeling?) add a little more milk – but only a little.

★ *VARIATIONS* ★

★ Drop teaspoonsful into cup cake papers or a bun tin and bake for 15 minutes.

★ Adding an egg makes this a richer cake. Adding a tablespoon of brandy makes it richer still.

★ For a **Miser's Christmas Cake** add $\frac{1}{2}$ cup of flour (brown or white) and 2 teaspoons of baking powder to all of the above and bake for 50–60 minutes in a moderate oven (375°F/190°C/GM5). Depending on the flour it may need more time (stab it with a cane skewer to test for doneness).

BASIC PASTRY

Pastry-making on board is a breeze; remember it's 3:1 flour to fat with just enough water to mix.

WHAT YOU NEED
(to line 2×6″ (15 cm) flan tins or make 12 covered mince pies)

Flour 1½ cup
Fat ½ cup
Water 3–4 tbsp
Salt

Simple as that.

WHAT YOU DO

Crumb the fat into the flour using the pastry blender (adding pinch of salt improves the flavour). Gradually mix in the water to make a dough. Knead lightly to get all the bits to stick together. If you have time and a cool place let the pastry sit for an hour (the best results happen when the pastry goes from cold to hot quickly). Roll out as desired and bake in a hot oven (425°F/220°C/GM7).

Cooking times vary with the size and thickness of the piece being cooked. Small tarts and pies take only 10 minutes, an (unfilled) 7–8″ (18–20 cm) pastry case about 12–15 minutes but a filled flan with lid can take 45 minutes. If you're making a filled pie such as a quiche it's often a good idea to make the case first and pop it in the oven for 10–12 minutes while you prepare the filling. Whip it out, fill and pop it back for another 20–30 minutes to cook the filling. This way you avoid the possibility of a soggy bottomed case which drops its load. It also gives you a quiet ½ hour to revive with your favourite nostrum or even clear up a little.

TIMELY TIPS

● Use plain flour for pastry; self-raising will work but it tends to bubble up and distort. If you store only plain you can always add a raising agent when the occasion demands (*see* below). This also makes life simpler as you need only keep unbleached white and brown for ordinary cooking and strong white and wholemeal for bread.

● For pastry, cakes and sponges, the raising agent is bicarbonate of soda which fizzes when it comes into contact with acidic ingredients. Here the gas bubbles are trapped by the sugar and fat molecules, with flour supplying the support. (Use 1 teaspoon of bicarb to 2 cups of flour.)

★ *VARIATIONS* ★

★ Adding a little cayenne pepper to the flour when making a shell for a savoury pie gives a nice bite to the pastry.

BASIC PASTA

Now you can try this or not, and I have to admit that I don't make pasta too often. But once in a while, the mood grabs me. If it should grab you too, here's what you do. (Did I hear someone say, 'Go lie down till the mood wears off'? Come now, where's your sense of adventure?) 'I make my own pasta,' announced modestly with lowered eyelashes wows them even better than making your own bread.

WHAT YOU NEED
(for 6–8)

Bread flour   2 cups
Oil   2 tbsp
Water   2 tbsp

WHAT YOU DO

Put about half the flour in a large bowl, drizzle the oil over and mix roughly. Add the water and mix to a soft dough. Gradually add the rest of the flour to bring the dough to a less sticky consistency. If it gets too stiff add the smallest amount of water; if it's too sloppy add more flour. Work the dough until it can be handled on a floured work surface. Now comes the hard work. This dough has to be kneaded like bread to develop the gluten's elasticity. So roll, stretch and turn the dough until it is smooth and springy. Put it away, covered, in a cool place for 30 minutes to 1 hour. Then roll it out fairly thin and cut to desired shape. Allow to dry out for another 30 minutes or so before cooking in plenty of boiling salted water.

TIMELY TIPS

● Letting the pasta rest after kneading makes it more amenable to rolling out flat or it'll fight you every inch of the way.

● Keep the surfaces well floured; work on a plastic tablecloth on the saloon table.

● You can cut the pasta with a blunt knife or a wheel cutter. Or if the pasta is well floured, roll it up and cut slices off which you can unroll and allow to dry.

★ *VARIATIONS* ★

★ Cut into squares and drop tiny amounts of filling (*see* below) into the middle before sealing into little parcels of whatever shape you fancy. Folding over into triangles is the easiest. Moisten the edges with water to effect a good seal or the contents will come out in the cooking. Crimp the edges with a fork.

★ Replace the oil with beaten egg to make egg noodles. The same sort of kneading required; cut as desired.

FILLINGS FOR RAVIOLI

Ravioli are tiny amounts of something savoury sealed into pasta envelopes:

● Cream cheese well seasoned with Cayenne or herbs, your choice.

● Pounded pumpkin seeds with anchovies, seasoned with pepper.

● Tiny mouthfuls of Cheddar or Edam.

● Breadcrumbs moistened with crunchy peanut butter.

ONION BREAD

The smell of this bread just out of the oven has been known to drive men mad. And quite a few women too.

WHAT YOU NEED
(for 4)

Onion 1 large or 2 small
Bread dough About $\frac{1}{3}$ basic recipe
Butter 1 tbsp
Flour 1 tbsp
Milk $\frac{1}{3}$ cup
Seasoning
Garlic salt $\frac{1}{2}$ tsp
Pepper $\frac{1}{2}$ tsp freshly ground
Poppy/sesame seeds To garnish

WHAT YOU DO
Slice the onion and taking $\frac{1}{4}$ of it slice that even smaller. Fold these smaller pieces into the dough until they are roughly distributed. Press the dough into a 7–8″ (18–20 cm) pie dish and

leave to rise till doubled. Meanwhile gently cook the rest of the onion in the butter and stir in the flour mixing well to cook it for 2–3 minutes, then add the garlic salt. Gradually add the milk to make the consistency of thick cream. When the dough has risen coat the top with the onion mixture. Sprinkle over the seeds if you have them, and bake in a moderately hot oven (375°F/190°C/GM5) for 30 minutes. Serve with soup or just tear it apart and slather with butter.

It makes a good snack with cheese and pickles.

BANANA BREAD

This is a very good way of using bananas that are practically running away, they're so ripe. The bread keeps well and is a good 'stayer' for Night-Watch rations and the first days at sea. Slice and spread with honey at tea time. It toasts well, too.

WHAT YOU NEED
(for 1 loaf)

Bananas 2 very ripe, mashed
SR flour 1½ cups
Sugar ½ cup
Margarine ¼ cup
Egg 1
Milk 1 cup or so to mix
Vanilla 1 drop or two, optional

WHAT YOU DO

Mix all the ingredients together with enough milk to make a loose dough. Pour into a well greased loaf tin. Bake in a moderately hot oven (375°F/190°C/GM5) for 50 minutes. Test with a toothpick for doneness.

TIMELY TIPS

● It sometimes takes longer but doesn't seem to come out any the worse; it should look golden brown with a crazed top. If you're doubtful, tip it out of the tin and pop the cake back in the oven upside down on a flan tin.

● If something goes wrong and it comes out a bit heavy, blame the barometer. Chop it in pieces and use it for a trifle with a good slurp of sherry, jelly and packet custard. They'll beat a path to your door.

● When cooked, a thick slice, sprinkled with cinnamon, toasted and topped with icecream makes a quick pudding.

Cakes

Cakes for eating afloat are better baked in a loaf tin as it makes them easier to slice. You may have to adjust the cooking time as a long narrow cake cooks faster than a fat round one; use the toothpick test.

Line your bun tins with fairy cake papers when using 'dropping' mixtures. This saves greasing the pans and washing up, and in the long run is cheaper on resources. Remember, your time is a resource: valuable, costly and given grudgingly. For some reason, non-stick pans stay non-stick longer if you don't use detergent on them. Loaf tins in particular, if treated from new like this, will only need dusting out after baking. It makes sense to have all baking utensils with non-stick linings.

A quick icing for that packet mix or store-bought cake you smuggled aboard is to moisten enough icing sugar with cream instead of water. This makes a cake topping which does not harden, and being so rich with the cream you can spread it thinner so it goes further. Flavour with a few drops of vanilla, instant coffee or lemon juice and colours if you want. Use it to sandwich plain biscuits together or biscuits that have succumbed to the 'marine environment'.

MRS KING'S SPICY CUP CAKES

Our dear friend Edith has never been to sea in her life and at eighty something has no intention of starting now. Her cooking, however, is a byword to legions. She spoiled us something wicked when we stayed at Croft Farm for a while, so I give you her recipe for cup cakes.

WHAT YOU NEED
(makes 18 cup cakes)

SR flour   1 cup
Sugar $\frac{1}{4}$ cup (3:1 white and brown)
Margarine $\frac{1}{2}$ cup
Eggs   2
Marmalade or honey   1 tbsp
Mixed fruit   2 tbsp
Milk   Enough to mix
Seasoning
Cinnamon   1 tsp
Mixed spice   1 tsp

WHAT YOU DO

Beat all the ingredients together thoroughly with enough milk (or water) to make a 'dropping' mixture. Spoon into cup cake papers. Bake in a hot oven (425°F/220°C/GM7) for 15 minutes. (If these last the day I'll be surprised.)

 *TIMELY TIPS*

● Using cup cake papers makes sense as they save greasing pans and washing them. I know you've got the residual paper, but it does screw up small.

★ *VARIATIONS* ★

★ I've made these with 85% wholemeal flour and I think they turned out better. They're not as light as with white flour, but you do feel you've had something to eat.

★ Skip the marmalade and sugar and substitute 1 tablespoon of malt extract and 2 teaspoons of powdered ginger. Use brown flour for super moist ginger cakes that keep well – if you hide them. Very good for sailing tummies.

★ Try ground cardamom in place of the cinnamon/mixed spice.

GINGER PARKIN

Good for sailing tummies.

WHAT YOU NEED
(makes 16 slices)

Plain flour $\frac{1}{2}$ cup
Oatmeal, medium   1 cup
Bicarbonate of soda   1 tsp
Margarine $\frac{1}{4}$ cup (or butter)
Treacle $\frac{1}{2}$ cup, or malt extract/golden syrup
Brown sugar $\frac{1}{2}$ cup
Milk $\frac{1}{3}$ cup approx.
Egg   1
Seasoning
Ground ginger   2 tsp
Cinnamon   1 tsp

WHAT YOU DO

Mix the dry ingredients together, except for the sugar. In a large pan gently heat the fat, treacle and sugar. Gradually add the dry mix, alternating with enough of the milk and beaten egg to give a fairly soft mix. Pour into an 8″ (20 cm) square non-stick tin and bake in a moderate oven (350°F/180°C/GM4) for 25 minutes, then a bit cooler at (325°F/160°C/GM3) for a further 25 minutes. Stick it with the toothpick to test for doneness. Turn out and cut into thick slices when cool.

Biscuits and scones

For biscuits and scones where you would roll the dough and use a pastry cutter to get those perfect circles they show on the colour pages of your magazine, why don't you start a new craze with SQUARE COOKIES. Roll the biscuit pastry out as thin as possible in an oblong shape and, using a dessert knife, i.e. blunt, or better still, a pastry wheel, cut lines 2″ (5 cm) apart the length of the pastry; then do the same the other way.

With a really thin biscuit paste you can sometimes get away with cutting it straight on the baking tray. The pastry wheel makes nice edges. For anything thicker than biscuits you will have to cut your squares first and then place them separately on the baking tray or they'll amalgamate on cooking. But you can still get more square biscuits on a tray than round ones. Don't flour the surface too much; it's better if the pastry holds still while you cut it.

Cutting dough in 2″ (5 cm) squares saves having all those funny shaped offcuts which never stand being combined and re-rolled. However, if your pride insists on round biscuits try pulling off a small lump of dough and forcing it down into a pastry cutter with the floured base of one of your flat-bottomed measuring cups – I told you they had many other uses. This gives nice round biscuits and no left overs – but you'll have two more items to wash up. Or you could try a burger press for larger biscuits. If you have access to a 'fridge, cool the dough (and this trick works for most biscuit doughs) for about an hour then put small blobs on to the baking sheet and flatten them with the bottom of a tumbler.

The tumbler won't stick if you butter it and dip it in sugar for each pressing. This method does mean hanging around another hour while the dough cools so you can't clear up, but you might want to try it some time. My philosophy, however, is to K.I.S.S. – KEEP IT SIMPLE, SAILOR. Keep it Square!

RICE COOKIES

No oven needed!

WHAT YOU NEED
(makes 24 slices)

Margarine $\frac{1}{2}$ cup
Sugar $\frac{1}{2}$ cup
Malt extract $\frac{1}{4}$ cup, or syrup or honey
Dates 1 8oz (225 g) packet, stoned and chopped small
Rice Krispies 5 cups
Seasoning
Vanilla $\frac{1}{4}$ tsp

WHAT YOU DO

Using your 'missionary' size pan over a low heat stir the margarine, malt extract, sugar and chopped dates till blended to a nice sticky goo. Add a few drops of vanilla if you like. Remove from the heat and gently fold in the Rice Krispies until they are coated with all the goo. (Now you know why I said a large pan.) Press into a well greased flat baking tin and smooth down firmly with a spatula to depth of about $\frac{3}{4}$″ (2 cm). When cool, cut into slices and keep locked in an air-tight bin/tin, or they'll fly away.

★ Press thinly into two 7″ (18 cm) flan tins and use as a base for cheesecake (*see* Janet's Easy Cheese cake page 132).

CHARLOTTE'S SCRUMPTIOUS SCONES

Charlotte sails with Rob in *The Yellow Banana* around the Orwell. These easy scones are just the thing for tea while waiting for the tide to retrieve you from Gunfleet Sands. Quick and easy to make as the kettle boils, you needn't even wait for the oven to heat up – it can go in even before the right temperature has been reached, just give it 5 minutes or so extra. My onboard oven has no thermostat – for the short time it takes to cook these scones I leave the oven on full blast.

WHAT YOU NEED

(for 4–6)

Plain flour   2 cups
Sugar   3 level tbsp
Fat   3 tbsp (butter or margarine)
Baking powder   2 tsp
Milk   Enough to mix

WHAT YOU DO

Mix all the ingredients in a bowl with enough milk to make a soft sticky dough using a rubber spatula. Turn out on to a floured board and knead roughly for a minute. Shape into a round 7″ (18 cm) or 8″ (20 cm) on a baking tray, and bake in a hot oven (425°F/220°C/GM7) for 15 minutes or so.

TIMELY TIPS

● Score the top with a knife, star fashion, 2, 3 or 4 times. This makes the scone break easily into 'ready' segments when cooked.

● Unsure if the scone is cooked? Take it out of the oven and, holding it with oven gloves, break it open at the score marks. It should look fluffy inside if done. If not, pop it back in the oven, without the pan, for another 5 minutes.

★ *VARIATIONS* ★

★ Throw in a handful of mixed dried fruit. Or add a teaspoon of ground mixed spice, or both. Use a proportion of brown flour (not bread flour). Form into individual scones. You could go mad, roll the dough to $\frac{1}{2}$″ (12 mm) thick, use cookie cutters to make neat little shapes and glaze the top with beaten egg. (Who's kidding whom?)

CHEESEY SCONES

WHAT YOU NEED
(makes 12 scones)

Flour   1 cup, brown and white, SR or plain
Fat $\frac{1}{3}$ cup (butter, margarine or whipped cooking fat)
Cheese   1 cup more or less, grated hard cheese or
other
Water   1 tbsp (that's all, don't be tempted to add more)
Egg   1 yolk (but sling in the whole thing if the white will
go to waste)
Seasoning
A good dash of cayenne or chilli seasoning mix
Salt   1 pinch

WHAT YOU DO

Throw the seasoning into the flour and, using your pastry blender, crumb in the fat, then toss in the egg yolk and cheese and mix well. Use the water to blend into a fairly stiff dough. (You may have to use your hands at this stage but the dough should be stiff enough not to stick, or use the rubber spatula.) Roll out $\frac{1}{3}''$ (8 mm) thick, cut through in 2" (5 mm) squares and lay in a greased or non-stick baking tray. Bake in a hot oven (425°F/220°C/GM7) for 10–15 minutes till golden and sizzling.

   *TIMELY TIPS*

● Look at them after 10 minutes to see if they look done (depends on thickness).

● SR flour makes a lighter scone. If using plain flour, roll thinner for a crisper biscuit.

● If you use a blander cheese than mature Cheddar add a little extra salt.

● This pastry makes an excellent shell for mild flavoured quiches, like leek or plain old egg.

JOY'S GOLDEN OATIES

To qualify for entry into this book, Joy claims to have sailed on the Isle of Wight ferry. Regardless of the validity of this claim these cookies would gain entry anywhere.

WHAT YOU NEED
(makes 18–24 squares)

Golden syrup   1 tbsp
Sugar   ½ cup
Butter   ½ cup (or margarine)
Rolled oats   1½ cups
Flour   ⅔ cup
Bicarbonate of soda   ½ tsp

WHAT YOU DO

Put the syrup, sugar and butter in a large heavy pan over a low heat and blend, stirring from time to time. While that's heating, mix the other dry ingredients together and add them to the syrup mix, turning it all over well to combine the two thoroughly. When well mixed drop walnut sized blobs onto a non-stick or greased baking tray and bake in a moderate oven (350°F/180°C/GM4) for 15 minutes. Lift off with a spatula and allow to cool on a wire rack.

★ *VARIATIONS* ★

I think these cookies are best just as they are but you might like to try some of the suggestions below. Add any of the following:
★ Grated coconut along with the rolled oats
★ Flaked almonds and almond essence
★ Glacé cherries, chopped
★ Almonds and cherries together
★ Sultanas
★ Cinnamon and ginger – about 1 tsp of each.

When adding the nuts – including the coconut – use a little extra syrup.

SHEILA'S MUESLI BISCUITS

Sheila sails *Oranmara* through the Hebrides with husband John. Knowing she was a school-meals supervisor and with a name like Beaton, I stood in awe. Meals afloat would hold no horrors for her, I thought. No, they don't. She simply 'vittals ship' with shop-bought long-life 'ready-meals'. She did offer these tasty biscuits, though, and ready-meals are worth a thought.

WHAT YOU NEED
(makes 24 squares)

Golden syrup 1 tbsp
Butter $\frac{1}{2}$ cup
Brown sugar 1 cup
Brown flour 1 cup
Muesli 2 cups
Baking powder 1 tsp
Seasoning
Mixed spice 1 tsp

WHAT YOU DO

Melt the syrup, butter and sugar in a pan, stir in the flour, baking powder, mixed spice and muesli. Line a 9″ (23 cm) baking tray with foil or greaseproof paper, pour the mixture into the tray and bake in a hot oven (400°F/200°C/GM6) for about 15 minutes. Allow to cool a little, then cut into squares and turn out.

TIMELY TIPS

● The cooking time varies with the thickness of the mix. Bake 20 minutes for a chewier biscuit or longer for a crisper one.

★ *VARIATIONS* ★

★ This is a heavier biscuit than Joy's Golden Oaties but will also accept the same variations like glacé cherries and almonds. Experiment and see which you like best.

★ Make a 'sandwich' with Gibstuedl (see page 129) as a filling. Bake for 20 minutes.

DIB'S PLAIN OAT BISCUITS

These are the quickest plain biscuits I know; very tasty on their own and excellent with cheese or other savoury spreads.

WHAT YOU NEED
(makes 18 squares)

Oatmeal $1\frac{1}{2}$ cups, medium
Oil 2 tbsp (any sort or margarine/butter)
Salt 1 tsp

WHAT YOU DO

Mix all the ingredients with enough boiling water to make a soft dough and roll out thinly. Cut into 2″ (5 cm) squares and lay them on a baking sheet. Bake in a moderately hot oven (375°F/190°C/GM5) for 10 minutes.

★ *VARIATIONS* ★

★ I made these with ordinary porridge oats the other day because I wasn't concentrating (so what's new?) and they turned out rather well being easier to roll out, but oatmeal was the original ingredient from Dib.

★ Sandwich two biscuits with cream cheese and a slice of pickled gherkin or sliced olive.

★ Bake the squares in a bun tin so they curve and, when cool, use as canapé shells; fill with anything, sweet or savoury. Easier than puff pastry.

DRINKS

The Quakers will tell you, 'Everything – in moderation' and now the doctors have decided that a glass of wine a day is positively *good* for you. So, if you're still reeling from the latest blast of the Skipper's usual subtle line of enquiry like 'What the blazes do you think you're doing with that warp/fender/sheet/anchor?' Just RELAX, put away your conscience and let him check the mooring while you try some of these Timely Tinctures.

PIRATE'S PUNCH

WHAT YOU NEED

White wine	Cinnamon stick
Rum	Honey
Lemon or lime	Whipped cream
Water	

WHAT YOU DO

Mix the wine and rum 2:1. Add 1 part of water and a sliced lemon or lime (you can use cordial if you have no limes). Heat gently with a cinnamon stick, add honey to taste, and top each glass with a blob of whipped cream (ordinary cream does nearly as well).

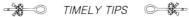 *TIMELY TIPS*

● This is a good one for a party as the wine – which can be any old gut-rot – and the water make the rum go a long way. You can throw in chopped fresh fruit if you like.

POOR PIRATE'S POSSET

WHAT YOU NEED

Cheap port	**Whole cloves**
Water	**Honey**
Lemon	**Mixed spice**

WHAT YOU DO

Mix 2:1 cheap port and water, heat gently with 1 lemon stuck with cloves plus ½ tablespoon mixed spice. Squeeze in the lemon, and let it float in the pan. Add honey (or brown sugar) to sweeten.

TIMELY TIPS

● One bottle of port with ½ bottle of water makes barely more than one litre (1¾ pints) – that's only 4 × ½ cups. Perhaps you'd better start off with 2 bottles of cheap port to save you getting up again. Double the spice while you're about it.

● Glass will hold liquid at a hotter temperature than you can drink it if it's prepared correctly; it's the sudden difference in temperature, cold to hot or hot to cold, that shatters it. If you sit the glasses in hot water and stand them to drain just before serving, you can safely ladle hot liquid into them.

PIRATE'S COFFEE

WHAT YOU NEED
(per person)

Strong black Coffee 1 cup
Cinnamon stick
Brown Sugar or Honey
Brandy $\frac{1}{8}$ cup
Double Cream

WHAT YOU DO

Add the cinnamon stick to the coffee and sweeten with brown sugar or honey. Add the brandy, stir and pour double cream on top.

CREW SAVER

WHAT YOU NEED

Yoghurt
Milk
Honey
Spice of your choice (see below)

WHAT YOU DO

Mix the yoghurt and milk 3:1, sweeten with honey, and add spice of your choice. Whisk until well blended. To be sipped slowly.

 *TIMELY TIP*

● Try ground cloves for a suspected cold. Cinnamon for chilblains. Mixed spice for damp socks. All three for a thick head.

CORPSE REVIVER

WHAT YOU NEED
(per person)

Milk 1 cup
Brandy $\frac{1}{8}$ cup
Honey 1 tbsp
Egg 1

WHAT YOU DO

In a jug put the milk, brandy, honey and egg. Whisk all till blended.

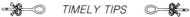 *TIMELY TIPS*

● Serve with dry toast for tender tummies.
● Can be heated very gently in a double pan so as not to cook the egg.
● NOT for the hypothermic, or omit the brandy.

GINGER TEA

WHAT YOU NEED
(per person)

Boiling water $\frac{1}{2}$ cup
Brown sugar (or honey) 1 tsp
Ginger (chopped root or dried) $\frac{1}{2}$ tsp
Fresh fruit juice (or long-life carton)
Full strength tea (without milk)

WHAT YOU DO

Pour the boiling water on to the sugar or honey and add the ginger. When the aroma has developed, top up with half and half tea and fruit juice; adjusting proportions to taste.

TIMELY TIP

● Nice drunk hot as tea but good also when cool. Good stomach queller, to be taken before, during and after sailing.

LEMON GRASS TEA

Lemon grass is a grass-like herb (available in the herb section of supermarkets). It has a distinctive lemon flavour and makes a soothing drink hot, or it can be allowed to cool.

WHAT YOU NEED
(per person)

Dried chopped lemon grass　1 tsp
Boiling water　1 cup
Cinnamon stick
Honey or brown sugar to sweeten

WHAT YOU DO

Infuse the chopped lemon grass in the boiling water with a cinnamon stick. Allow to brew and sweeten with honey.

DIB'S HONEY CUP

WHAT YOU NEED
(per person)

Boiling water　½ cup
Milk　½ cup
Honey　1 tsp
Cinnamon stick

WHAT YOU DO

Pour the boiling water on to the cinnamon stick and allow to draw. Add the milk and honey.

 *TIMELY TIP*

● This is a good and economic alternative to tea as a regular drink. It also has the advantage of being caffeine-free for those trying to kick the habit.

★ *VARIATIONS*

★ The cinnamon stick is an enhancement and can be omitted.

HOT GINGER POSSET

WHAT YOU NEED
(per person)

Preserved root ginger   (see chapter on Seasoning)
Boiling water
Milk
Honey

WHAT YOU DO

Crush the ginger in your garlic crusher. Place the crushings in a cup, half fill with boiling water and allow to 'brew'. Top up with milk. Sweeten to taste with honey.

   TIMELY TIPS

● While you're at it, crush plenty of ginger and store it in a screw-top jar for other uses. Or put it through the blender ashore.
● Do the whole thing in the microwave, 2 minutes on full.
● For a de luxe version, use all milk. If using dried milk fill the cup to the top with hot water and add milk powder.
● This drink is excellent for frail sailing tummies as well as for soothing an attack of The Bloat (overeating).

MULLED WINE

WHAT YOU NEED
(makes 6 glasses)

Red wine   1 bottle (cheap)
Ground cloves   1 tsp
Ground cinnamon   1 tsp
Brown sugar $\frac{1}{4}$ cup
Slices of lemon/orange/apple or other fruit to hand

WHAT YOU DO

Over a very low heat blend together the spices and sugar (or honey or malt extract) in $\frac{1}{4}$ cup of water. When well blended add the wine and stir to mix thoroughly. Throw in a couple of slices of fruit to garnish and turn off the heat.

 *TIMELY TIPS*

● This brew must not boil.

● Serve in glasses (*see* p. 159 for safe preparation of glass for hot liquids), though it's nearly as good in mugs. Great with mince pies, great for a party – great any darned time.

● A sovereign remedy for incipient madness; in cases of suspected relapse, double the dose. Continuous application could give immunity – to anything.

● In view of its efficaciousness, it might be as well to make a double batch.

INSTANT HOT CHOCOLATE DRINK

WHAT YOU NEED

Drinking chocolate   1 tub
Coffee creamer   1 tub
Instant dried milk   1 tub

WHAT YOU DO

Take equal parts of each of the above and mix thoroughly. Use by adding very hot (but not boiling) water to 2–3 heaped teaspoons of the mix. Sweeten to taste.

 *TIMELY TIPS*

● You will find that a 9 oz (250 g) tub of drinking chocolate holds just *under* 2 cups and a 9 oz (250 g) tub of coffee creamer holds just *over* 2 cups. The 7 oz (200 g) drum of dried skimmed milk also holds just over 2 cups. The simplest thing to do is tip all three into a large strong plastic bag, twist the neck tight and 'massage' the contents until well mixed before decanting the mix back into the three containers. Remember to relabel the other two.

The slight discrepancy in proportions makes little difference to the end result and you can adjust the proportions further if you like. You can mix the whole lot in a bowl but the chocolate dust flies up your nose and you're still faced with getting the mix back into narrow containers plus the bowl to wash. The plastic bag technique takes care of all this. If all your crew like the same amount of sweetening add 1 cup or more of sugar to the mix to make life easier still.

SEASICKNESS

It's a curious thing that when you enquire if a sailing person suffers with seasickness the answer is invariably in the negative. On the other hand, they know old What's-His-Face who was never on the bridge without a bucket. The tellers of these stories don't know the meaning of the word themselves, can't understand it, and consider it could be malingering on the part of the sufferer. They will relate, as per Jerome's *Three Men in a Boat* that '... sometimes it was he and the captain ... sometimes he alone, who were not ill', to the point of death it would seem. Amazing. But the human gizzard is a strange and unpredictable organ.

My dear Aunt Olive was renowned for her honey and the management of its makers. On one occasion she was asked to assist with a particularly wayward bunch of bees that had swarmed somewhere up country and were proving difficult to discipline. Up she went with veil and gaiters and the bees were eventually persuaded to behave properly. Not, however, before some of their party had managed to penetrate my aunt's armour and express their rage.

She, poor soul, was taken to the house of her host and made to rest in the sumptuous drawing room. After a short while she felt she was on the verge of disgracing herself and called for a receptacle. The flustered hostess, casting about for a suitable vessel, lit on the silver salver gracing the sideboard and thrust it under my aunt's chin.

But Olive was gently born and, at seeing her reflection, her sensitive nature recoiled at soiling such a fine piece. Her heaving stomach promptly seized and the fit passed; my aunt recovered and honour was saved – along with the salver.

Now, whether you feel you are as finely bred as my aunt and that carrying a piece of rare silver smithery will dissuade your nausea is something only you can judge. Personally, I take pills.

Stugeron was developed as a motion sickness controller for pilots in space. Unlike most other types of motion sickness pill which depress the signal receptors in the brain and can make you feel sleepy or below par, Stugeron works differently. It thickens the fluid in the tiny canals of the inner ear so that the little hairs that wobble about as your head moves don't wobble about quite as much, sending fewer confusing signals to the brain. The advantages are that your other faculties are not affected, you remain alert, well and confident.

A positive mental attitude also goes a long way to keeping the dreaded feeling at bay. Being occupied with jobs requiring a degree of concentration 'takes the mind off it' quite literally, as the brain can only handle so much incoming information at one time and will block less demanding signals. (Hence the reason you missed the weather forecast on the car radio because you were so busy navigating your way around an M25 junction.)

But the real battle with seasickness begins several days beforehand with attention to diet, cutting out the heavy proteins, i.e. red meats and fats, and replacing them with light proteins – eggs, cheese and lentils. Boosting these with high-fibre carbohydrates like brown rice and pasta, wholemeal bread and jacket potatoes gives the system a chance to clear and settle. Adopt a routine of four or five smaller meals during the waking hours. This is far easier for the stomach to cope with than waiting until you're starving and then stuffing yourself full. It needs a bit of discipline and organisation but what would you prefer?

A suggested routine for, say, the first four days (last two ashore, first two afloat) might be:

Dawn	0600–0630	Tea, cereal and toast with marmalade (no butter or margarine).
Mid-morn	0930–1000	Eggs in one form or another with brown bread, tea/coffee. Fruit.
Lunch	1400–1430	Main meal of the day. Low fat savoury and dessert. Tea/coffee.
Tea	1800–1830	Scones with fruit and jam, cake, tea.
Supper	2330–2400	Toasted sandwich, fruit and tea.

The dawn meal can be split into a further two starting with just tea and cereal and half an hour later, toast and more tea. Lunch should be substantial as the main meal of the day but with smaller portions so the total food intake is the same as would be consumed with the standard three meals. Supper can be shared with changing watches during the handover period. It helps a lot to turn out to do your stint at the helm with a comfortable feeling of having eaten a little. The secret is not to eat too much; feeling full can be uncomfortable in a seaway. Remember: Little and Often.

It's the cook's duty to see that the Night-Watch Nosh Box has a supply of good nibbles, slices of fruitcake and biscuits (without chocolate). Hot soup or tea in a thermos which is easily accessed from just inside the hatch (*see* chapter on the Galley) is a great morale booster at 0230 when you feel the edge of the world can't be far away.

Going without food for more than three hours at the beginning of a voyage is not wise as it allows the stomach to dwell on itself. By eating little and often – and mostly light proteins and carbohydrates – blood sugar is kept up which keeps tiredness and despondency at bay. Claire Frances found a high carbohydrate diet including cakes and honey guarded against the dreaded lassitude brought on by seasickness.

If seasickness becomes a reality, then after the spasm of vomiting has ceased, there are two courses of action: keeping the patient occupied or making the patient rest.

If the patient is not too distressed and the weather reasonable then they are better in the cockpit, possibly taking the helm with a compass course or a landmark to follow. Studying the horizon really does work because the brain can make sense of these signals and has a steady reference point to relate the other signals to. If out of sight of land and there is sun or enough to make a shadow then checking the boat's direction when on the correct compass course against a shadow line on deck will give a good guide for helming. At night, putting a star in the rigging or watching the moon is another good game for keeping the mind busy. Just remember that shadows and stars move and the reference points will have to change periodically. This is not meant to be a treatise on navigation but a simple way of occupying children or crew who may be suffering.

Patients who have been suffering to a point where they are very distressed and cold should be made to rest below. Although it is sometimes difficult to persuade the sufferer, lying down does ease the motion. The most comfortable place to be on most boats is on the cabin sole, because it is low and in the middle of the boat where the movement is least. I once spent three days wedged in between the lockers and the saloon table legs, and I didn't care how many times I was stepped on. Only hardy types like my sister can handle the forepeak, where you get tossed like a pancake as the mattress leaves the bunk every time the bow plunges into another trough.

Get the patient to change into dry clothes if necessary and empty the bladder before tucking him (let's have a bit of sexism here) into a sleeping bag in a bunk with a lee cloth or cushions to stop him rolling about. A hot-water bottle can be very comforting as people often feel cold when seasick. But remember, if the patient is truly hypothermic (really cold, barely conscious) they must be allowed to warm up on their own, however odd that may seem, well wrapped in blankets/sleeping bag.

Seasickness causes dehydration and the lost fluids must be replaced, but little by little so as not to create a sloshing sensation inside. A personal stereo can help to divert the mind until sleep claims it. We found a personal stereo very useful on long passages used with tapes or the radio. The only trouble is that the listener can't hear you calling for help on deck!

Diet for the seasick crew is a matter of what takes the fancy but again the rule of Little and Often is kinder to a tender tummy. Definitely NO ALCOHOL. Dry toast to nibble and sips of warm (not hot) tea or Ginger Tea (*see* chapter on Drinks). Appearance helps when the spirits are low; and you may think it's silly but I've not met any sufferer yet who didn't appreciate, with a wan smile, having his toast and Marmite/Eggy Bread cut into soldiers.

SUGGESTED DIET FOR SUFFERERS

- Crackers, rusks, crispbread and rice cakes
- Toast (sorry, no fats) spread with a scrape of honey or sprinkled with Spiced Sugar (*see* page 45), Vecon (*see* below), Bovril or Marmite
- Eggy Bread, dry fried or toasted under the grill (*see* page 78)
- Miser's Muesli (*see* page 126)
- Thick Onion Soup with Poached Egg (*see* page 59).

DRINKS

● Hot Ginger Posset, Crew Saver, Corpse Reviver, Ginger Tea (*see* chapter on Drinks)

● Vecon (from a health food store – *see* page 44) is a vegetable paste, delicious spread on toast or bread. A spoonful in a $\frac{1}{2}$ cup of very hot water topped up with cold makes a warming savoury drink.

Drinks for the seasick should be warm, not hot, as the sufferer may have lost the sensation in hands and lips and could scald themselves with a hot drink. Also, if spilt, there is less of a hazard. Sipping through a straw is not recommended as it can shoot hot liquid to the back of the throat.

MISCELLANEOUS

As already observed, peeling back the shrouds of mystery around some previously baffling enigma can sometimes expose it as just plain commonplace. Now, this may not always be a wise practice. One does not necessarily want – or need – the explanation to a lot of things; indeed, some things remain better wrapped in veils of intrigue.

For instance, my husband marvels at the way I appear to skitter through life, always seemingly on the brink of one minor disaster or another, from which he has to rescue me – naturally. He cannot imagine how I ever managed to scrape through without coming to a sticky end before he happened along. The answer is, of course, that in common with a lot of other women I juggle the elements in my life like a circus performer with plates on sticks, always rushing from one to next, convinced that if I move fast enough, like Einstein tells us, time truly will stand still. It's quite simple really. Well, if he ever rumbles me I'm lost, but I still have one or two tricks up my sleeve and hope, with a bit of luck, to keep him fascinated for some time to come. All this leads me on to the last section of this book which contains all the bits and bobs I couldn't find a home for elsewhere.

● Francis Chichester used to drink a small glass of sea water every day, claiming it as a mineral supplement. Just don't try it on your way down the Bristol Channel; I think you might get more supplement than you bargained for.

● Use the white of egg – lightly whipped – on burns, sunburn and nappy rash. The albumen in the white brings quick relief from the stinging, and the temporary 'skin' formed as the white dries prevents blisters if the burn is not too bad and helps to guard against infection if the skin is broken. Use NO oils, fats or creams. Do NOT puncture blisters – the bubble formed keeps pressure off the raw flesh underneath and provides a sterile environment for the growth of new skin. Seek further medical aid if necessary.

● Keep a small bottle of hydrogen peroxide (10 or 20 vol.) from your chemist in the medical box. It's an excellent skin steriliser for scratches, though it stings a bit.

● Keep a small spray can of Burneze in the galley drawer. It brings instant relief to minor burns and scalds. Make sure everyone knows it's there and that they replace it – you may need to find it in the dark.

● I bet the Post Office never heard of this one. A covered dish in a large padded envelope (or some bubble wrap) will keep the contents hot (or cold) for an hour or more. It will also do service as an ice bucket.

● Never let coffee boil on making or reheating; it ruins the taste and colour. If making filter coffee let the water come just off the boil before pouring over the fresh coffee grounds. Keep ground coffee in the fridge to preserve freshness.

● Borax mixed with a little sugar will attract and kill cockroaches. But then you have to find out where they've crawled away to, to die. Better is a Roach Motel, a little box which they go into but don't come out of. Try your hardware store.

● Rust marks can sometimes be removed with a little paraffin on a cloth. You can try a lemon on things you don't want smelling of paraffin. Naval Jelly (from chandlery stores) contains phosphoric acid and works well on cloth as well as the more usual metal and plastic.

● Clear silicone sealant has many different uses. It will stick almost anything to just about anything else. It will patch holes in rubber gloves. Repair leaky yellow wellies when they start to craze at the ankle. Use it to tack small cables out of the way. Hold the trailing edge of the curtains to the bulkhead with a thin slick along the seam. The merest wisp will stop material edges fraying and a little more will make a non-slip coating for the bottom of mugs, thump mats, etc.

● Blood spots on clothing can be removed with hydrogen peroxide. Do not wet the cloth but apply a little H_2O_2 directly onto the stain when it will fizz white while there is still blood present. Leave for a few minutes and repeat the application till no fizzing occurs. Rinse the area in cold water.

● If you carry your fruit and vegetable shopping in string bags, you can give them a quick dunking in sea water to get rid of any nasties before getting back aboard.

● Plastic carrier bags are useful for all sorts of storage but the handles soon pull through if hung on a hook. Try passing the hook of a plastic coated clothes hanger up through the handle hole of the bag and then turning the top of the bag over the rest of the hanger like a cuff. You can bend the shoulders of the hanger down to fit the size of the bag. This is a useful form of gash bag as the hanger will keep the bag pulled tight shut. Use one in a hanging locker for socks/undies/gloves. Ashore, this Tidy-All can have 100 uses. Polishes, dusters, damp cloths, etc. will follow you around the house hung on your belt.

● Remember: if you just can't cope – open a couple of cans: Heineken or Stella, your choice.

INDEX